Gardening at the Shore

GARDENING AT THE SHORE

Frances Tenenbaum

Photographs by Jerry Pavia

TIMBER PRESS

Frontispiece: In a garden designed by Wolfgang Oehme, *Salvia* ×*sylvestris*, achilleas, and *Rudbeckia maxima* are open to the wind, protected to some degree by ornamental grasses. Feldman garden, Martha's Vineyard, Massachusetts

Published in 2006 by
Timber Press, Inc.
The Haseltine Building
133 S.W. Second Avenue, Suite 450
Portland, Oregon 97204-3527, U.S.A.

www.timberpress.com

For contact information regarding editorial, marketing, sales, and distribution in the United Kingdom, see www.timberpress.co.uk.

Printed through Colorcraft Ltd., Hong Kong

Library of Congress Cataloging-in-Publication Data

Tenenbaum, Frances.
  Gardening at the shore / Frances Tenenbaum ; photographs by Jerry Pavia.
     p. cm.
  Includes bibliographical references and index.
  ISBN-13: 978-0-88192-793-1
  ISBN-10: 0-88192-793-7
  1. Seaside gardening--United States--Pictorial works.   I. Pavia, Jerry. II. Title.
  SB460.T46 2006
  635.9'5--dc22   2006008576

A catalog record of this book is also available from the British Library.

CONTENTS

ACKNOWLEDGMENTS   6

PREFACE: THE SAME BUT DIFFERENT   8

INTRODUCTION: THE COASTS   14
Pacific coast ~ Northeast coast ~ South Atlantic coast

A SPECIAL KIND OF GARDENING   30
Wind and windbreaks ~ Planting in sand ~ Invasive plants

GARDENS AT THE SHORE   66
Pacific Northwest ~ California ~ Northeast ~ Southeast

ADVICE FROM SEASHORE GARDENERS   94
Cady Goldfield ~ Ann Hunt ~ Dorie Eckard Redmon
George Guthrie ~ Valerie Easton ~ Judith Larner Lowry
More Advice

PLANTS FOR SEASHORE GARDENS   108
Trees and shrubs ~ Vines ~ Perennials ~ Grasses

VIEWING COASTAL GARDENS AND HABITATS   158

EXTENSION SERVICES   163

USDA PLANT HARDINESS ZONE MAP   165

BIBLIOGRAPHY   166

INDEX   169

ACKNOWLEDGMENTS

One of the great pleasures of writing a book is meeting a whole set of new people with new ideas. Another is reconnecting with those you knew in the past. This book has presented me with both, and I am grateful to all of them.

Jerry Pavia is a talented photographer whose pictures I have used in many of the books I've edited. When he agreed to shoot new gardens for this book, I knew that half the battle was already won.

Of course I could never have written this book without the help of other gardeners, especially those on other coasts, who gave so generously of their time and knowledge. Although I've been gardening on Martha's Vineyard for many years, and although I've even written and edited books and articles related to this kind of gardening, I have had no direct experience other than my own.

To these friends from the past and new acquaintances (whom I have come to consider good friends) my great appreciation; their contributions appear throughout the book: Cady Goldfield, Ann Hunt, Dorie Eckard Redmon, George Guthrie, Valerie Easton, Steve Schramm, Phyllis McMorrow, Judith Larner Lowry, and Nan Sinton.

To the gardeners who allowed us to photograph their gardens: Bob Dash, Trudy Taylor, Gretchen Feldman, Susan Epstein, Sally Robertson, Terry Camiccia, and all the others not named here.

I appreciate the patience and good humor of the Timber Press team, who certainly have had much easier authors to work with than an editor-turned-author who thinks she knows it all. Little haloes over your heads. And, as always, to all my colleagues at Houghton Mifflin who have been such a pleasure to work with lo these many years.

—FRANCES TENENBAUM

I would like to thank Frances Tenenbaum for asking me to be her photographer for this project and for opening her home to my wife and me when I was photographing on Martha's Vineyard. For me it was a great honor to work with Frances.

I would also like to thank all the homeowners who allowed me to photograph their gardens, usually at a very early or late hour. It is only at those magical hours that the best light appears, often for the briefest of times. A big thank you to the following designers who went out of their way by spending many hours with me showing me their work: Lew Whitney of Roger's Gardens Colorscape, Christopher Rose of Christopher Rose Architects, Jean Rothrock of Waccamaw Landscaping, John T. Hoff of Oakleaf Landscape, Steven Schramm and Jean Turner of Island Gardens Landscape, and Gary Ratway of Digging Dog Nursery.

I would also like to thank my assistants, Trish Bryant and Jan Rose, for without their attention to detail in selecting images for possible use in this book and their undertanding of who I am as a photographer, this book and none of the others I've done would have been possible.

And most important, a heartfelt thank you to my wife, Ingrid, for traveling with me for part of this work, for supporting me in all my creative efforts, and for the unconditional love she sends and seeds my way.

—JERRY PAVIA

Preface : THE SAME BUT DIFFERENT

A garden on San Juan Island in Washington state, with a mixture of native plants and locally adapted nonnatives. Hood/Logan garden. Design by Steve Schramm

"The newcomer to the seaside must observe carefully his own site and those of his neighbors before making elaborate plans. He must learn all he can about the exposure of his property, how the storms affect it, and what plants in adjoining areas have shown the greatest endurance."

—Daniel J. Foley, *Gardening by the Sea from Coast to Coast*

A successful seaside garden on the Pacific Ocean may look like a garden five miles inland from the shore, but making it will be different. It won't look like a seashore garden off the coast of Massachusetts, but making it will be pretty much the same.

In other words, gardening within the sight and sound of water calls for similar techniques wherever you are, but because the climates and the hardiness zones are different, the plants will mostly differ from coast to coast—as well as from your waterfront to your inland area. If this sounds so obvious, I can only confess that it took me many years and many failures to learn what works and what doesn't in a seashore garden. I came to my Martha's Vineyard garden with only the experience of gardening in a typical New York suburb and it didn't occur to me that there was a very real difference between the two.

I still remember buying a small dawn redwood, *Metasequoia glyptostroboides*, and planting it where I could watch it from my bedroom window. I particularly like the story of how a clump of this presumably extinct tree, common when the dinosaurs roamed the earth, was found in China in 1941 and propagated for modern gardeners. What no one ever said was that this was a good tree for wind, salt, and sand. Even if it had been, planting a tall slender tree by itself in those conditions would have killed it.

Formal elements, like this geometrically trimmed boxwood hedge, can have a place in seaside gardens. Dickson garden, DeBordieu, South Carolina. Design by Jean Rothrock

A garden right on the water in South Carolina. The dramatic palmettos are the perfect foil to the low junipers and yaupon hollies.
Bell garden, Pawley's Island, South Carolina. Design by Jean Rothrock

In Myrtle Beach, South Carolina.
Creagh garden

Bright pink rhododendron blooms
shine against the blue *Ajuga reptans*
in this garden on Whidbey Island
near Seattle. Blue garden

The chapters that follow are filled with the variations and eccentricities of gardening techniques, and advice of experienced seashore gardeners who have overcome obstacles. Their suggestions for the best seashore plants are far and away the surest road to your success in your endeavor.

My hope is that this book will save you from expensive and discouraging mistakes. And that you'll learn to enjoy the challenges and appreciate the results of gardening at the shore where, as Daniel Foley wrote, the "colors of blossoms and foliage appear to glow brighter, the tints and shades are more distinct. The blues are bluer and the pinks are pinker and dew-drenched flowers in the morning light have a freshness that is not found in gardens inland."

This home and garden, right on the main street, overlook the harbor. Campbell garden, Martha's Vineyard, Massachusetts. Design by John F. Hoff

Miscanthus sinensis 'Yaku-jima' grows with *Verbena bonariensis* by back steps on a foggy morning in Lynn and Charles Meyer's garden on San Juan Island, Washington.
Design by Steve Schramm

INTRODUCTION : THE COASTS

A view along the California coast.

It will probably not come as a surprise to anyone who lives on the edges of the North American continent that more people every year are moving from the interior to the coastal states, 3600 people every day, according to a climate study sponsored by the National Oceanographic and Atmospheric Administration.

A cypress at sunset on the California coast.

Not everyone in coastal states can see or hear the water, but for those of us who can, this makes the often difficult job of gardening more than worthwhile.

In this chapter, I'll make an attempt to describe briefly these coastal areas, their similarities and their differences. But these descriptions, at best, have to be generalities. A long stretch of natural coast isn't like a freeway, the same mile after boring mile. Your house along the seashore may be fronted by a wide sandy beach or you could be overlooking the water from a high cliff.

As any gardener knows, the *general* rule for deciding which plants will survive where we live is governed by the plant's hardiness—in other words, how well it will survive the coldest days of winter. We judge this by looking up our geographical region in the United States Department of Agriculture Plant Hardiness Zone Map. That's a pretty good rule, but it's of only limited usefulness at the seashore. Of course you're not going to have much luck planting a semi-tropical plant in Maine (although you might be able to do it on the Northwest coast). But since

HARDINESS ZONES

In the back of this book, and most other books on gardening, you'll find a map of United States Department of Agriculture (USDA) Plant Hardiness Zones. To see individual zones more closely, try the interactive online version of the map at www.usna.usda. gov/Hardzone/ushzmap.html. The zone or zones you see after each plant description in "Plants for Seashore Gardens" in this book are related to that map.

The numbers tell you one thing only: the average lowest winter temperature in the zone. It doesn't tell you *anything* else. This is just a very broad estimate and it doesn't take into consideration such significant details as whether your land is at the top or bottom of a hill, caught in a windy tunnel, or whether winter lasts two months or four. In other words, it's a general guide. You can find out your zone just as easily by asking at a good local nursery.

And once you know your zone, you can forget the map. Most gardeners like to "stretch" their zone by placing a plant in a protected spot (a microclimate) or by adding protective mulch in winter. And seashore gardeners realize that their gardening climate probably differs from what the map tells you anyway. It tends to be warmer at the shore and you can quite likely grow plants that wouldn't be hardy enough to flourish a couple of miles inland. On the other hand, even though it's warmer where you are, you may not be able to grow those inland

seacoasts are often warmer than inland areas at the same latitude, you may be able to grow plants that would otherwise be too tender for your geographical latitude. Plants that grow five miles inland will be in the same hardiness zone as your shore garden, but may not survive at the seashore because they aren't tolerant of wind, salt spray, blowing sand, and infertile soil.

The rough environment of sandy beaches and dunes is a fragile one for plants, and one easily disturbed, even destroyed, by human activity. But along all our coasts, these are the areas of greatest appeal to visitors and residents. Throughout these regions homes and resorts are built as close to the shore as possible, often located on unstable slopes or even on recently created sand dunes.

PACIFIC COAST

The Pacific coast I cover in this book ranges from California through Oregon and Washington, including Puget Sound. Many of the same plants will grow from the northern coast of California, through the Pacific Northwest, some even as far north as Alaska. Whether the coast is marked by broad sandy beaches or rocky cliffs and headlands, the maritime climate is one of relatively mild dry summers, cool, rainy winters, and persistent summer fogs.

PACIFIC NORTHWEST

An interesting University of Washington report by scientists working with the Climate Impacts Group, an interdisciplinary team that is part of the Joint Institute for the Study of the Atmosphere and Ocean, describes the Pacific Northwest as having three distinct coasts:

the shores of Washington's inland waters of Puget Sound and the Strait of Juan de Fuca

the Pacific Ocean coast itself

the shores of the Washington and Oregon estuaries fronting the ocean.

Puget Sound is a large, many branched fjordal system where storm energy is tempered by the inland location. (Although the winds may be tempered, Steve Schramm, a landscaper who works on Puget Sound

Knowing your zone will help you make choices when you read plant lists or plant descriptions. If the plant's hardiness zone is 6 and you live in northern Maine's zone 5, you may not want that plant. So what about the zones given with each description? I think you should assume that's the *general* zone limit for that plant. Not the seashore-adjusted limit. When you are proficient at this kind of gardening, you can see what your neighbors are growing or your local nursery is selling, and stretch the boundaries of your zone too.

Roses, lavender, and bougainvillea grow near palm trees in a Laguna Beach, California, garden on the Pacific Ocean. Design by Roger's Gardens Colorscape

islands, talks about the sixty-mile-an-hour winter winds that blast through his gardens.) The shores along Puget Sound are mostly narrow beaches that are inundated at high tide. Substantial portions of the central and south shoreline have been "armored" with bulkheads and sea-walls to protect industrial development and residential properties. This coast is the most intensively developed in the region, with expensive

The Pacific Northwest climate includes regular fogs in summer, which can add an air of mystery to the garden. C. Meyer garden, San Juan Island, Washington. Design by Steve Schramm

bluff-top or beachfront trophy homes and suburban areas. Along the eastern shoreline, the homes are mostly full-time residences; along the western, mostly vacation homes.

By contrast, the Pacific coast is open to the full force of storm-driven waves. The Oregon coast and Washington's north coast are bordered by steep bluffs and small beaches; Washington's south Pacific coast is characterized by broad sandy beaches. Much of the land in Washington is held by Olympic National Park and five Indian tribes. Oregon's Pacific coast is a mix of undeveloped shore, small towns and cities, and expensive vacation homes, condominiums, and resorts. In both states, tourism is a major economic development. For example, the city of Ocean Shores in Washington has 3300 permanent residents and 1.5 million visitors each year.

A garden on San Juan Island in Washington, overlooking the Strait of Juan de Fuca. The cinnamon-barked madrona, *Arbutus menziesii*, is one of the gems of the local coastal flora. B. Meyer garden. Design by Steve Schramm

Because beachfront property is so highly prized, much of the private development along the Pacific Ocean coast has been built directly on the shore. In recent years large developments and hotels have been added to the previous mix of small one-family homes. Continued armoring of shore-side property to protect it from erosion—or even to be nothing more practical than a landscape amenity—also has a negative effect on the quality of the beaches. The third Pacific coast is made up of the many small estuaries and the two large coastal estuaries on Washington's south coast. These are shallow and as much as 50 percent of the area consists of mud flats. Farming, fishing, and shellfish aquaculture are important areas of development rather than home construction.

For those of us who believe the Pacific Northwest is the best place in the world to garden—and the only place in the United States where you can grow wonderful English plants—writer Valerie Easton throws some dark light on this picture. Writing in *Horticulture* magazine, Easton points out that Seattle (zone 8) is right next to Alaska in the number of days each year over 86 degrees; just one in seven. And winter is dark; Seattle is at the same latitude as North Dakota and Newfoundland. It's also wet, with so much rain from October to March that hills can slide into the ocean.

What makes the Pacific Northwest such an ideal place to garden is primarily the moderating climatic influence of the Pacific Ocean. It rarely gets below 20 degrees and more plants are smothered in soggy soil than freeze to death. Gardeners here understand that the cool spring will keep bulbs blooming, but it's the warm fall days that invite you into the garden.

CALIFORNIA

Summer fog gives coastal gardeners in California advantages that inland California gardeners can only envy, says plantswoman and author Judith Larner Lowry, a native plant nursery owner, and she goes on to describe varied types of California coastal regions:

Bluff edge This is where you get spectacular views and sleepless nights worrying about erosion and landslides. No place for lawns or any plants that require watering.

Coastal scrub More gardens in these plant communities—north and south—than any other. Follow the general advice for seashore gardening.

CALIFORNIA'S FIFTH SEASON

California's "Fifth Season," writes Judith Larner Lowry in *Gardening with a Wild Heart*, is August through October, "that long, luxurious warm spell with no rain." The gardener's tools are "a hammock, a book, and a glass of lemonade. With no moisture, the weeds (most kinds) will be at rest as well, so the gardener can make his leisurely way through the garden, watching pollinators at work, watching flowers turn slowly to seed."

Redwood forest Plantings are limited because of dense shade.

Mixed evergreen forest This, Lowry says, makes up in livability what
    it lacks in grandeur. Fire and safety regulations should be
    your first landscaping rules.

The exuberant Pacific Ocean
garden at Harbor House Inn in Elk,
California.

The instability of coastal cliffs and the potential for fire must be ad-
dressed on the California coast; the gardener starting out to plant a wind
shelter needs to be particularly careful not to exacerbate these conditions. Two trees once recommended for this purpose have been found
to be unsuitable. The Monterey pine, *Pinus radiata*, can grow too tall
where the soil is deep or the water table high and create dangerous fire
ladders. The Monterey cypress, *Cupressus macrocarpa*, can make an excellent hedge if it is faithfully pruned twice a year. Left to itself, it shoots
up to become an unmanageable tree. Sally Robertson, whose garden is
presented in this book, discusses how she manages these trees, which she
considers to be "coastal weeds."

The ability of Californians to grow virtually anything makes it hard to resist growing too many things. Aesthetically your yard may look more like a jungle than a garden, but growing the wrong things can cause more serious trouble than that to your senses. Lowry has said that a large proportion of her landscape business is removing plants that were put in with the idea that they would control erosion.

NORTHEAST COAST

The Northeast coast ranges from the northernmost tip of Maine, where the plant hardiness zone is 5, to the Washington, DC, area where it is 7. It's colder along this coast than any other coast in the country, with the greatest range of temperatures—bitter cold winters and very hot summers. Around Boston, the Gulf stream, which has warmed the shores of Cape Cod and the Massachusetts islands, Rhode Island, Connecticut, New York, and New Jersey, veers off toward England leaving northern Massachusetts and Maine's 3500 miles of diverse coastline shivering behind.

In some parts of the Northeast, garden plantings have to contend with the super-aggressive common reed, *Phragmites australis.* Hewitt garden, Long Island, New York

Narcissus growing on the north fork of Long Island. Design by Connie Cross

But cold is not the only limiting factor for plants. Rapid freezing-thawing cycles, common on the Northeast coast, are more deadly than longer stretches of cold weather. Protective snow cover is melted away to expose plant roots to killing freezes. Northeast storms (nor'easters), with high winds, driving rain and/or sleet and snow, are most common between November and April, but not uncommon in summer.

Patrick Chassé, a landscape architect from Mt. Desert Island in Maine, says that hurricanes, gales, squalls, storms, and other combinations of high winds, heavy rain, and tidal surges are the most serious natural catastrophes on this coast. The wind carries salt spray as much as several miles inland where it burns plant leaves. Chassé thinks that much of the winter damage is due to wind, not low temperatures alone.

Another feature unique to the weather on this coast is our very cold, late spring and very long warm autumn. Martha's Vineyard is one planting zone warmer than Boston, and it is also about seventy miles south. So it's no surprise that we can grow some plants there that won't survive in Boston. What is surprising in spring is to see everything blooming in Boston while the Vineyard is still brown and bleak. The answer is the

A garden on the south shore of Long Island, with a path running down to the Atlantic Ocean. Catmint, Russian sage, and Japanese irises contribute a wealth of purples. Design by Bob Venuti

Atlantic Ocean, whose vast cold winter water affects the temperature on the island, making our springs cold and late. The effect of the ocean's warm summer water is to extend the gentle temperature into late fall.

Still another consideration if you live on this Northeast coast has to do with exactly where you live. This coast and the Southeast coast pretty much run into each other. If you feel you are borderline geographically, you may be able to use plants from either hardiness zone. The easiest way to figure that out is to see what your local garden center is selling—or what your next-door neighbor is growing.

WHAT'S THE DIFFERENCE?

On the website gardenweb.com a lively exchange took place in 2004 when a Long Island, New York, gardener asked about the biggest differences, pro and con, between inland gardening and gardening by the sea: "Mine has to be dealing with the wind. It's a rare day when it isn't blowing . . . and it always does some kind of damage . . . . My 4th of July rose is a prime example. I don't think it has a leaf on it without some windburn . . . . Typically [it's] 5 to 10 degrees cooler here than even a mile inland. . . . On the positive side planting season is just about all summer long [and] I don't have as many pests as others I read about."

A gardener from Mystic, Connecticut, answered that the difference was the sun—"or at least I believe that is the name for the large red/orange ball some people report seeing in the sky. We see very little of it here. I painted our sunroom with a color called 'Mystic Pewter' . . . . there's always an overcast sky. Well, not always but much of the time."

Another New Yorker felt differently about sun. "My home is surrounded by sand and reflection off the sand during summer can really fry plants. . . . Notwithstanding morning mists, afternoon fogs, and the humidity [this] necessitates water, water, water."

From Maine: "It is more humid here; powdery mildew is very much at home. . . . Generally, winters are more mild, though last year . . . I lost a lot of very hardy things—*Miscanthus*, *Dictamnus*, *Akebia*, 'Sweet Autumn' clematis, bulbs fared poorly, too. *Buddleia*, *Caryopteris*, hardy hibiscus, and roses suffered big hits, or folded completely. I've lived here for 13 years now . . . and I've only just begun to understand, let alone massage, the subtleties of the climate that dictates success/failure in gardening!"

From the Massachusetts shore: "Less stress on the plants . . . and summers cool and 'English'. For falling asleep in a hammock, the sound of the waves beats the sound of the highway every time." A fellow Massachusetts gardener boasted that in early spring he found a spot where he could hear both the peepers and the waves.

SOUTH ATLANTIC COAST

Although gardeners may think of the Southeast as the romantic land of magnolias, azaleas, and Spanish moss, this is not the kind of gardening we're talking about here. Four states contribute areas to this coastline—a bit of Virginia at the north, North Carolina, South Carolina, Georgia, and the northeast coast of Florida. For the most part, these shores are on the string of heavily populated barrier islands that extend a thousand miles between the Atlantic Ocean and dry land. Major resort and housing areas are the Outer Banks of North Carolina, where the winds of Cape Hatteras are legendary; off the Lowcountry, on Hilton Head,

Live oaks near a lawn that was built on land raised above a marshland. Quantz garden, DeBordieu, South Carolina. Design by Jean Rothrock

A boardwalk from the house goes over *Spartina pectinata*. Vineyard home, Kiawah Island. Design by Christopher Rose

Few woody plants are as majestic—
or provide as much protection from
wind—as the southern live oak,
Quercus virginiana. McClary garden,
DeBordieu, South Carolina

between Charleston, South Carolina, and Savannah, Georgia, and the sea
islands off the Georgia coast.

The south Atlantic coast has a humid, subtropical climate with hot
summers, warm winters, and rain all year. Land on the ocean side of the
islands is sandy, on the bay side generally marshy.

Glenn Morris, writing in the *Taylor's Guide to Seashore Gardening*,
says these islands are fundamentally alike, "great piles of sand shaped by

the forces of wind and wave." They range in length from less than a mile to more than twenty. A few are broad enough to have high land that essentially is not the seashore. But the sandy oceanfront property is both the least stable and the most desired location. On the frontal dune, he writes, the only plants that thrive are American beach grass, sea oats, and pressure-treated lumber. If you want to grow anything to protect your property, one or both of those native grasses is your best bet.

Behind this front dune, and to some extent protected by it from wind and salt, you'll find plants growing in the thin soil and blazing sunlight. Here's the place to begin. But before you do, the first thing to do is to plant a windbreak—or have one built.

Dorie Eckard Redmon, a garden designer and horticultural specialist, worked for years in the Lowcountry, including Beaufort and Hilton Head, a region that is fast being taken over by gated golf course communities.

Gardening is a challenge in these areas, she says. "The Lowcountry is a semi-tropical environment. Our limiting factors are afternoon sun, salt in the air and soil, shore winds, months of high temperatures and high humidity, and year-round populations of biting insects and all of the plant pests you can think of."

A boardwalk leads to the Atlantic Ocean over sand dunes on Kiawah Island, South Carolina. Legasey home. Design by Christopher Rose

A SPECIAL KIND OF GARDENING

Even sturdy *Quercus virginiana* can have its growth distorted by ocean winds.

"It shapes new forms, probes new habitats, stirs up unrest and foments evolution," wrote naturalist Lyall Watson, in *Heaven's Breath: A Natural History of the Wind*, and the wind's effect on vegetation is obvious: "Trees growing on cliffs and windy shores are permanently swept leeward." As poet George Seferis wrote, "Pines keep the shape of the wind, even when the wind has fled and is no longer there."

Large conifers protect this garden right on the coast at Mendocino, California. Moss garden. Design by Gary Ratway

WINDS AND WINDBREAKS

In his classic book, *Gardening by the Sea*, Daniel Foley said, "Writing about wind is like writing about air," and added that it isn't possible to say too much about its damaging effects. Although he credits the dramatic shapes of seaside plants to "wind pruning," Foley goes on to describe the damage that these same winds and wind-borne salt and sand can do to plants.

It isn't only hurricane-force winds that affect our gardens, although they do so in sudden destructive ways. I remember arriving on Martha's Vineyard on a Sunday in August of 1991, a week after Hurricane Bob. As I drove from the ferry to the outward area of the island, I seemed to have entered a strangely foreign land. Although it was a warm summer's day, I was surrounded by completely brown vegetation. Even miles inland, the wind had borne enough salt to burn all the foliage, as well as to down trees all over the island.

On Long Island, Colorado blue spruce
act as a buffer to other plantings.
Design by Connie Cross

Although I've been lucky enough never to feel the brunt of a serious hurricane, Bob gave me my fifteen minutes of fame. A few weeks
after it hit the island, I was talking to columnist Anne Raver by phone,
as I described how I was simultaneously raking oak leaves and cutting
the flowering lilac branches. The next day's *New York Times* featured this
weird juxtaposition as its page two "Quote of the Day."

Yet even a Cassandra couldn't design a garden guaranteed to survive a hurricane. It is the storms that batter our coasts on a regular
basis, and the everyday winds, the constant breezes that make island life
so comfortable; even the lighter summer winds that cool us off while
our friends in nearby mainland cities are sweltering—these winds affect
coastal plant life and they, not the wild, boundlessly destructive Bobs,
Ritas, or Katrinas, are the winds we can actually do something about.

A BRUSH WITH THE WINDS

Wind off the coast damages plants in a number of ways other than the
obvious one of toppling trees and branches. The most severe damage
comes from the salt carried by the wind. Long-term exposure to salt in
the soil causes stunting: shortened limbs and small leaves. The wind also
blows sand that abrades leaves and causes shoots and branches to die back.
Your best strategy for dealing with winds is twofold: choose salt-hardy
plants *and* create windbreaks to block the passage of salt-laden wind.

Wind affects your plants even at a range away from the ocean where
you hardly notice the effect of the salt it carries, (though we probably

On top of a very windy hill, the
whole house acts as a windbreak for
a Martha's Vineyard garden, allowing
an unlimited variety of perennials to
grow. Epstein garden. Design by Keith Kurman

The purple leaf plum on the right,
Prunus cerasifera 'Vesuvius', helps to
shelter this northern California garden.
Moss garden. Design by Gary Ratway

HURRICANES

I wrote this chapter before Katrina hit New Orleans and the Gulf coast in 2005. Nothing I could have said here would have made the slightest bit of sense in the face of that tragic storm. I had planned to write about gardening on the Gulf coast, but with that coast literally gone, I couldn't bear to talk about the gardens that no longer exist. On the other hand, hurricanes are a constant threat in the South, and if you live in hurricane territory, I hope the suggestions here will help your garden survive.

If a hurricane is projected for your neighborhood, painter Robert Dash, whose humor and know-how is featured later in this book, suggests that you get out your pruning shears and do some preventive surgery on your small garden trees and shrubs. The ones you can reach.

Specifically, he advises cutting back long lateral branches. If they are unpruned, a strong gale could catch them and overturn the whole plant. Roots already loosened in the soaking wet soil won't be strong enough to brace the plant.

But don't attempt this on a tree you can't safely manage with your feet on the ground. And don't do it as a general precaution, just because some day a hurricane could strike your area. This kind of pruning may save a tree in a hurricane emergency, but it isn't going to make it more beautiful. Allen Sistrunk, director of Mounts Botanical Garden in West Palm Beach, Florida, says he has seen palm trees pruned to a Q-Tip. Palms are trees that can easily ride out a hurricane on their own. Pruned they are ugly and actually weakened by loss of their leaves. He warns homeowners that when tree companies show up before a storm to prune palm trees, it's a racket.

Although wind is a constant on a seashore garden, it would be foolish for most gardeners to plan a garden that is resistant to a hurricane that may never come. Still if you live in Florida, or other coastal communities where hurricanes are distinct possibilities (and projected to increase as the climate continues to warm), it makes sense to keep that in mind as you plan your seashore garden.

The 2004 hurricanes—Charley, Frances, Ivan, and Jeanne—that swept through Florida, one after the other, uprooted and damaged even the most storm-resistant trees like the native live oaks. In her *New York Times* article about the damage, Anne Raver interviewed botanic garden directors and nursery owners about the best and worst trees to grow.

Unfortunately, they said, people who lost the trees protecting their camellias and other valuable shade-loving plants rushed out to buy quick-growing replacement trees. Since even the fastest-growing trees wouldn't provide shade in time to keep those plants from dying, they were actually just purchasing fodder for the next hurricane.

Although no plant is 100 percent storm proof, some are better than others. Palms are about the best: appropriate for the region, low-maintenance trees, and quite resilient in the face of a storm. They can bend and sway in the heaviest winds without breaking. Other good trees are bald cypress, *Taxodium distichum*; palm cypress, *Taxodium ascendens*; southern magnolia, *Magnolia grandiflora*; live oak, *Quercus virginiana*; yaupon holly, *Ilex vomitoria*; river birch, *Betula nigra*; white cedar, *Thuja occidentalis*, and trident maple, *Acer buergerianum*.

Fast-growing trees tend to have weak wood. Popular trees planted for shade, but bad for hurricane country, include hickory, *Carya ovata*; laurel oak, *Quercus laurifolia*; Chinese elm, *Ulmus parvifolia*; golden rain tree, *Koelreuteria paniculata*, and camphor tree, *Cinnamomum camphora*. The last two are invasive and weedy in the South.

should). My small house faces due north, with a great view of the water, although I am probably a quarter of a mile from the shore. The ground falls away steeply on the north side, so that I can't build a fence or plant a windbreak that will be tall enough to protect a garden. But the *Rosa rugosa* I planted behind little shingles on that steep slope grow beautifully, and I garden elsewhere.

On the south side, the house protects the garden from the wind and that is where I grow trees and bushes and flowering plants. No surprise, so far. But it's a small area and in order to have much of a garden, I wanted to plant on the east and west side of the house. I don't know how many years it took, or how many plants I lost, before I finally realized that the only way I could have a garden is if I established windbreaks. If this is confession time, I need to add that some of the trees and shrubs I tried to grow on the unprotected side of my house would have shown you how ignorant I once was—but of course they promptly died so the evidence is gone.

MAKING WINDBREAKS

While a windbreak can be made of many things and can be of almost any height, it is essential that the barrier be high enough to interrupt the prevailing wind. According to California native plant nursery owner Judith Larner Lowry, a hedge of shrubs and small trees twenty feet high will protect a six-foot-tall man standing fifty feet away. The denser the hedge, with smaller shrubs in front and behind it, the better the protection. Even a fairly low shrub-tree border about ten feet high, and composed of a variety of bushy plants interspersed with deciduous ones, is effective.

Writing in *Horticulture* magazine, Bob Polomski of Clemson University said that wind speed and turbulence are reduced on the leeward side for a distance of thirty times the height of the hedge. In his estimate a ten-foot-high hedge will give some benefit 300 feet away. It seems awfully generous to me, but I'm not the expert. He also said that a hedge is better than a solid wall; solid walls and fences may seem like an obvious answer, but a not-so-obvious drawback is that they can create turbulence as they force the wind up and over the fence. Polomski states that a 60:40 ratio of solid to open barrier is ideal in reducing both the speed and turbulence of the wind because deciduous shrubs and trees keep 60 percent of their windbreaking function even when leafless.

In Mendocino, California, a garden is nestled below the protection of a tall hedge of evergreen *Teucrium fruticans*. Design by Gary Ratway

Native viburnum and wild grape vines protect a bed of astilbe in a Massachusetts garden. Sametz garden, Martha's Vineyard, Massachusetts

Thymes, dianthus, lavender, and lady's mantle thrive in container and patio plantings near the sea. Netters garden, Long Island, New York

A hedge of *Ligustrum japonica* is a windbreak for *Miscanthus sinensis* 'Variegata' in this South Carolina garden. Dickson garden. Design by Jean Rothrock

Daylilies are among the most accommodating perennials for seaside gardens.

A Southeast planting of *Quercus virginiana* and *Ilex vomitoria* 'Nana' is simple but effective. O'Bryan garden, Prince George, South Carolina. Design by Jean Rothrock

A sturdy wooden fence is designed to let some wind pass through the upright boards. Fruchtman garden, Stinson Beach, California

Enough of all this mathematics. The answer is obvious. If you want to grow anything but the hardiest wind- and salt-tolerant plants, you need to have or create a windbreak. The lay of your house and your land may dictate what kind of windbreak you'll have. If your house is your windbreak, you won't have to plant or build anything, but just look for the quietest places in the lee of the house. If you want to build a windbreak, or have one built, there are a few things to remember. The most important is to make sure the fence posts are strong enough to keep the fence firm in the sand so it is able to stand up against the wind. A flimsy barrier is no barrier at all. The second feature, as Polomski said, is to make breaks in the fence to allow some wind to go through. I saw an amazing hedge on a large windy estate while researching this book. It was at least fifty feet long, composed of four rows of ten-foot-tall privet shrubs. Very high maintenance. A much easier informal planting of groups of salt-tolerant trees and shrubs is generally considered the best long-term solution to the problem of wind.

Behind a simple fence, the gardener makes even delphiniums survive, although admittedly she grows them as annuals. Taylor garden, Martha's Vineyard, Massachusetts

You can scarcely see the fence, but it protects an elegant planting. Camiccia garden, Bolinas, California

You can give your plants serious protection from the wind and still get a delightful keyhole view as this Martha's Vineyard garden shows. Campbell garden. Design by John F. Hoff

In northern California, a hedge behind doubles the protection of the stone wall. *Limonium perezii* provides long-lasting color in USDA zone 9 and higher. Design by Roger's Gardens Colorscape

A lattice fence and clipped boxwood enclosures protect smaller garden areas in a Southeast seaside garden.
Kelley garden, Kiawah Island, South Carolina. Design by Bill Maneri

A garden right on the beach is possible if you put low plants against a low protective wall—and you don't mind staking taller plants. Newport Beach, California. Design by Roger's Gardens Colorscape

Lush and colorful container plantings on a fenced deck in the Pacific Northwest also make whale-watching more comfortable. San Juan Island, Washington. Design by Steve Schramm

Although somewhat challenging to train and maintain, the form of espalier known as Belgian fence —here executed with pear trees— makes an elegant fence even if it doesn't stop much wind. Shank garden, Amagansett, New York

SALT

Annual sunflower (*Helianthus annuus*) is one plant that can take the salt-laden wind off the water, seen here on San Juan Island, Washington.

The presence and effect of wind on a garden by the shore is easy to see, to feel, and to understand. If the wind were not carrying salt, it wouldn't have much deleterious effect on our gardens beyond bending tree trunks and breaking branches. It's the salt that is carried by the wind that does the real harm. In extreme weather conditions, such as a hurricane, the salt spray can affect plants as far as fifty miles inland. But gardens that experience the most damage from salt are those located within 1000 feet of the shore. Our gardens.

Although all sorts of plants are affected by salt spray, the effect on trees is by far the most significant. Obviously it's easy, if necessary, to replace a perennial or even a shrub. Moreover a tree that isn't killed may be deformed to the point that it is no longer attractive in the landscape. In that connection, the USDA Forest Service conducted an interesting study of the salt-tolerance of the street trees in the city of Virginia Beach, Virginia. As a tourist destination, Virginia Beach expects its street trees to enhance the city's beauty. What the forestry people found was discouraging for the city but a useful lesson to seashore gardeners like us.

Salt and trees generally don't mix. So-called salt-tolerant plants can withstand 40,000 parts per million (ppm) of saltwater. The Atlantic Ocean contains more than 32,000 ppm of salt. What this means is that one or two heavy deposits of salt, or several moderate ones, can easily exceed the tree's level in its leaves and stems.

Whether inherent in the soil, blown in as sea spray, or splashed on as roadway de-icing material, salt can damage trees in two ways. Salt within the soil affects the soil structure and can hurt the tree's roots. But the most significant damage comes from the ocean spray that covers the above-ground parts of the tree.

Starting with a list of salt-tolerant trees hardy in Virginia's zone 8 and then eliminating trees that were too large, too messy, or otherwise inappropriate for a city planting, Virginia city streets turned out to be hostile environments for the most salt-tolerant trees studied.

By the end of the first year the loquat, *Eriobotrya japonica*, had been heavily damaged. So had the golden rain tree, *Koelreuteria paniculata*; the sweetgum, *Liquidambar*; and the lacebark elm, *Ulmus parvifolia*. Nor'easters from August through October had defoliated the trees before they became dormant, resulting in partial releafing. That new growth was killed by cold in November and December, leaving dead terminal buds and twigs and sparse foliage the following spring. Several early spring nor'easters repeated the first year's scenario and by the end of the second year all the trees were dead or too deformed to be acceptable. One of the most widely considered salt-tolerant trees is the honey locust, *Gleditsia triacanthos*, but neither this, the often touted southern magnolia, *Magnolia grandiflora*, nor the sweet bay magnolia, *Magnolia virginiana*, did well at all.

Whether or not we grow any of these trees, there's an important lesson in the Virginia Beach test. And that's to water our trees—and other garden plants—after a storm. Obviously this is not practical for a city to do, but unless your property is too large to be manageable, the best thing you can do is to wash your plants with fresh, unsalted water from a garden hose. If it's not possible to do that, when you see dead and broken branches next spring, you'll know where they came from.

Salt spray—the good news

Not all the effects of salt spray are harmful. As I have mentioned elsewhere, I am sure the absence of mildew on my phlox and my lilacs is a direct result of the salt in the air. In her book *Gardening on the Eastern Seashore*, R. Marilyn Schmidt adds roses, hollies, and Austrian pines to my short list. Even beach plums, she says, produce fungus-free fruit at the beach, where inland they are prone to brown rot fungus. On the other hand, as gardeners in cloudy, foggy beach locations have complained, mildew can be rampant in those climates. Certain vegetables, Schmidt points out, like turnips, beets, celery, kale, and asparagus, absorb more water in the presence of a small amount of salt and grow more lush.

Low-growing thymes, catmints, and heaths are among the more salt-tolerant ornamentals. San Juan Island, Washington. Design by Steve Schramm

This garden manages a seamless transition from ornamentals growing in improved soil to native vegetation in sand.

PLANTING IN SAND

When it comes to setting out new plants, we gardeners at the sandy seashore undeniably face special obstacles. If ours is a vacation-home garden, we probably must do our planting at the least desirable time of the year, in the heat of summer. What compounds the problem, and makes it somewhat different from that of vacation homeowners at a lake or in the mountains, is that the constant elements at the seashore are sun, wind, and burning sand, all of which have a dehydrating effect on plants. Even the foggy or rainy days, which the vacationer deplores but the gardener occasionally relishes, are of only temporary help (although they are certainly the safest days for planting).

Virtually all of the planting suggestions and tricks described here, some of them quite unorthodox, are designed to overcome the drying effect of the seashore environment. Naturally, you won't need to follow all suggestions for every plant; some won't be appropriate and some won't be necessary, especially if you can arrange to plant in the spring or fall. And if what you read here sounds like a lot of trouble, think of the advantage you have over other gardeners: digging in sand is child's play.

START WITH SMALL SPECIMENS

Three years after we put in a dozen *Rosa rugosa*, six large and six small, they were all about the same size. While the bigger ones were accommodating themselves to their new homes, the smaller ones were catching up. Small plants are easier to install, more likely to survive, and can stretch your plant budget considerably. When I first started wildflower gardening, not many nurseries carried seashore plants. You still probably won't find them at a garden center, but as natural gardening has taken hold, you can order them from nursery catalogs. Also, as you'll discover in this book, many cultivated garden plants are hardy in sand, salt, and wind.

IMPROVING THE SOIL

Even though seashore plants grow in pure sand or the thinnest sandy soil imaginable, it is almost always a good idea to add compost, composted manure, peat moss, or other organic material when you plant. This will not only give the roots a good head start, it will retain water as sand itself will not. Oddly enough, planting right at the shoreline is somewhat easier than in the dry sandy dunes farther inland simply because

Rosa rugosa and beach grasses grow in pure, unimproved sand.

Ice plants and wild grasses grow in the sand near the Pacific Ocean at Bodega Bay, California.

Salvia leucantha, lavender, Mexican feather grass, and blue oat grass grow in the sand at Stinson Beach, California.

the groundwater level at the beach is closer to the surface and the air is damp with spray. Naturally, this is of no help with plants that are intolerant of groundwater salt or salt spray.

PLANT DEEP

Forget everything you ever learned about setting plants at their natural level and plant them deep, several times deeper than you ordinarily would. This is especially important in the case of trees and shrubs, and long-stemmed perennials, which should be buried right up to their top growth. For this good advice I am grateful to William Flemer III of Princeton Nurseries and author of an excellent book, *Nature's Guide to Successful Gardening and Landscaping,* who explains that the poor water-retention quality of sand means that the oxygen necessary for root growth can also penetrate deep into sand. By taking advantage of this knowledge, you can give your new transplants the benefit of a cool, wet root run without causing the roots and stems to rot as they would in wet soil. It also helps that you don't leave so much of the plant above ground to be battered by the wind.

PLANTING A DUNE

Dunes play an essential role in the stabilization of coastal communities. On barrier islands, as well as mainland beach communities, dunes are the first line of defense for homeowners whose houses are at or near the sea. In most communities these days, dunes are protected by state or local environmental rules, and it is important before planting anything on a dune to check with your community environmental office first. Nothing is easier today than finding out what you are and are not allowed to do on a sand dune. Simply type the words *sand dune laws* and the name of your state into your computer search engine, and type variations on that until you get the answers you are looking for. By adding "Florida" to "sand dune laws," I got a useful essay.

The most widespread dune grass, native to the East Coast and the Great Lakes, is *Ammophila breviligulata*, American beach grass. In dune restoration in these areas, that is the grass that is generally used; it can be bought in large quantities, often from the local dune-building site. This is the best grass for dune-building and restoration because, unlike these other approved grasses, it can be bought in large quantities of small plants.

Other locally approved beach grasses:

California and Pacific Northwest Native rye grass, *Leymus mollis* (also called *Elymus*). Don't use any form of *Ammophila*, which is invasive on the West Coast. Check a website to see if *Leymus* can be bought as seedlings.

Southeast *Ammophila breviligulata* plus *Panicum amarum*, panic grass, or bitter switchgrass. A clump-forming, dune-stabilizing beach grass native from Connecticut to Florida and Texas. 'Dewey Blue' is a handsome cultivar that grows 3 to 4 feet tall. It is noted for its powder blue foliage and fountainlike form. Zones 2 to 9. *Uniola paniculata*, sea oats, is an endangered species, protected against even picking in Florida. Well worth planting for its salt tolerance and long roots that go down to fresh water. Zone 7

How to plant a dune

Seedlings may be purchased from nurseries or from a local dune restoration committee. They are usually sold in bundles of fifty or a hundred stems. These figures refer to *Ammophilia breviligulata*; availability of other seedlings should be requested from the seller. Seedlings may also be dug up from your own property.

Step 1 Open a hole in the dune (or dune-to-be) 12 inches deep with a pointed stick. Place two stems, root down, in the hole. If they are not planted 12 inches deep they may dry out or be blown out by the wind.

Step 2 Make the plant holes 18 inches apart, and the rows between the holes also 18 inches apart, but staggered to prevent erosion.

Step 3 Press the sand down firmly with your foot and water the seedling in well.

Step 4 Although it is not essential, you may fertilize with nonchemical fertilizers, and mulch with natural mulches at the time of planting.

Use sand fencing to keep people off the dune. To add to the trapping of sand, you can put sand fencing at the base of the dune; support the fencing with 4 × 4 wooden posts spaced ten feet apart. Put the sand fencing on the landward side of the posts so that a storm doesn't uproot the posts. And make sure to add a pathway over or around the dune to keep people and boats from destroying the grass when they go from the beach to your house.

MULCH

Mulch, mulch, mulch! Since water will evaporate off the surface as well as leach down through the sand, mulching is one procedure you should never skip. It can also retard weed growth.

Mulch at the bottom of your planting hole as well as at the top, making sure that the bottom mulch is covered with a layer of soil or sand-and-peat mix. When I started gardening on what was an inland sand dune, I had no soil or compost on the property, and not a lot of money to import them. At the suggestion of a Martha's Vineyard nursery owner, I used crumpled up, soaking wet newspaper as a bottom mulch. It worked very well, but as with any mulch be sure to cover it with a layer of sand, or sand and soil, so the roots have something to grow into. After your bottom mulch has served its first function, that of helping retain moisture, it will eventually decompose and improve the sandy soil.

Mulch can be had nearby, naturally—especially seaweeds—or, clearly, you can buy your mulch. The variety of materials used for commercial mulch seems to expand every year. I certainly haven't tried them all, but the one I really don't recommend is wood chips. They take too long to break down, especially in the dry salty air of the shore, and I dislike their look. Another to avoid is peat moss. It is great if mixed in the sand or soil to make it richer, but if spread on top of soil it draws the moisture out of the soil and makes a dry, impenetrable layer so rain is not likely to get through.

FERTILIZING

Never use a dry chemical fertilizer on seashore plants, least of all in the heat of summer and when you are transplanting. You needn't fertilize at all when planting, but a weak solution of liquid fertilizer is helpful. To be extra safe, wait a few days before doing anything. Once a natural planting is established, there is no need to fertilize. However, if you want to do so, bear in mind the porosity of the sand and its surface heat. These two factors should tell you that it is both safer and more effective to apply two half-strength doses of liquid fertilizer than to give one dose at full strength.

WATERING

Like deep planting, this is another instance in which you are usually better off using a technique that is frowned upon in environments where the soil is heavy and water-retentive. One good initial soaking may be

shoulder, I like to think I am an Aran Islander, not a city dweller landscaping her summer house.

Salt-marsh hay Another wonderful mulch and soil improver is salt-marsh hay, which is cleaner, much lighter, and therefore much easier to handle than eel grass. It's also a prettier mulch where that is important. As the name indicates, this is the hay from salt-marsh grasses, which, very much like seaweed, is washed up onto the shores of the marshes. You can lift it in great sheets, so take a number of large plastic leaf bags when you go collecting and you will always have a supply on hand. Like all biodegradable organic mulches, the hay will eventually decompose to help condition the sandy soil. I find that it decomposes much faster than eel grass, which makes it better or worse, depending on whether you are more interested in having a mulch or a soil conditioner. I always want both, and over the years I have never found that I had too much of either.

Composted bark serves as a mulch in a Pacific Northwest garden. Hood/Logan garden, San Juan Island, Washington. Design by Steve Schramm

all you need to start a plant in clay, loam, or mucky earth, but here, especially on a slope, it is not enough. The excess water quickly leaches away and, if you are planting on a hillside or a dune, will create gullies. For the same reason, an untended sprinkler can be damaging to a sandy site. After the first good soaking, the best method, I find, is the hand-held hose. Be sure to saturate the ground, but as soon as the water starts run-

ning off, stop. In hot weather, new plantings may require two or more waterings a day. Naturally, the more mulch you have used, the better off they will be.

PLANTING A HILL

Setting out plants on a steep sand dune or a hill made of builder's sand, such as that created by changing the grade around a newly built house, has its own special problems: the mere act of digging a hole for the plants is likely to set off a small landslide. You can't—or certainly shouldn't—walk up and down on the hill, and if it is large enough and steep enough, you'll have to find a way to reach the plants without putting your weight on the loose sand. My solution, which wasn't very graceful, was to lie down at the top and work as far as I could reach. This was actually easier than reaching up from the bottom, which was also necessary to finish the job.

For the actual planting, I found my solution at the town dump, in the form of a pile of shingles. The advantage of shingles is that they are thin at one edge and thick at another, which makes it possible to tap them deeply into the sand without setting off a small avalanche in the process. Be sure to place your wood across the face of the hill, so you don't channel the water down into gullies. For the same reason, stagger your shingles. I was gratified to read an article on the plants of Block Island, off the coast of Rhode Island, by horticulturist Richard Churchill. On visiting a small truck gardener, he was amazed to see that all the seedlings were protected by a little wall of shingles. The first time in fifty years, wrote Churchill, that he had ever seen such a thing.

Leave about one-third of the shingle above ground, put eel grass or hay above the shingle, and dig your hole above that. Gently! Don't dig a wide hole if you can avoid it, but do dig a deep one, since your aim is to get those roots going quickly to stabilize the loose sand. Be extremely generous with mulch. In a year or two, or whenever plant growth has covered the shingles, you can pull them out or break them off at ground level. Anywhere else they would decompose, but the salty seashore air tends to preserve the uncovered wood. (A visitor thought my just-planted hillside looked like a cemetery.) The best "first" plants for an interior dune, even one composed entirely of builders' fill, is

A mature hillside garden on Puget Sound is lush with pink heather, prostrate rosemary, *Erica carnea* 'Springwood White', and *Amelanchier ×grandiflora*. B. Meyer garden, San Juan Island, Washington. Design by Steve Schramm

beach grass—which, of course, is the obvious choice for a seaside dune. One of its great virtues is that on a very steep hill, you don't even have to make a real planting hole; just poke your sharp trowel down as far as you can and quickly tuck the root and as much of the grass blade as you can into the crevice. The deeper you go and the more you get below ground, the better off you are.

SAVING THE DUNES

If your land includes or borders on a dune, you owe it to your own and your community's environment to protect those dunes. If your property runs down to the water, building a dune is the most important thing you can do to save your land.

Sand dunes are a natural barrier against the destructive forces of wind and waves. They exist wherever the coastline is edged in sand. They protect the lands behind them against the rages of ocean storms, and they move and grow with the weather. As the wind blows sand against them, if there are roots and stems to catch the sand, the dunes grow taller and more protective of the land behind them. To get to our local ocean beach at Gay Head on Martha's Vineyard, we have to climb the path to the top of a dune to reach the beach below. Over the years I have blamed my increasing difficulty climbing the dune on advancing age—until I saw that the dune has actually grown so high that even youngsters have discovered a way to get around it.

The alternative to a dune covered with protective plants is a sand pile that blows away or is washed over by the sea. But height alone is not

Residents of Pawley's Island, South Carolina, reach their beach without harming the dunes.

A boardwalk on Kiawah Island, South Carolina, makes it possible to get to the beach without damaging the dune grasses.

EXPOSURE BELTS

Helianthus debilis

In research on plants for the shore, you will come upon the term "exposure belts." Unlike the hardiness zones, these are not standardized. Some suggest useful general rules for seashore gardens, while others are specific to protecting or creating sand dunes.

R. Marilyn Schmidt, in *Gardening on the Eastern Seashore*, offers these categories:

Belt I An area in which plants can tolerate full exposure to wind, salt spray, and windblown sand as well as sand in the soil.

Belt II An area where partial protection exists. Fences and hedges may furnish protection for plants in this belt.

Belt III The protected area. Plant should have well-developed root systems, be small enough so that their loss, if it occurs, will be financially minimal. They need to be well watered and mulched.

For dune preservation, the delimitations are more specific. Although you will need to use plants that are native or hardy in your part of the coast, these exposure belts from the Florida Department of Environmental Protection offer good guidance anywhere:

Fore dune This piece of beach is characterized as a low, wind-deposited dune that is sparsely vegetated with the hardiest of dune-stabilizing plants. In Florida these would include railroad vine, *Ipomoea pes-caprae*; and dune sunflower, *Helianthus debilis*.

Dune crest This, as the name implies, is the highest dune behind the fore dune. The major plants are the native dune grasses. In Florida, this would include sea oats, *Uniola paniculata*, which state law protects from picking.

Sabal palmetto

Back dune This is a more stabilized coastal dune covered with a dense thicket of salt-tolerant shrubs. It is also the most rapidly disappearing plant community in Florida because it is prime real estate for residential and resort development. The back dune originally grew in a continuous band along the Atlantic. Now it grows in isolated broken stretches between developed areas. Among its native plants are live oak, *Quercus virginiana*, and cabbage palm, *Sabal palmetto*.

SAND LOVER

Beach grass, whose botanical name, *Ammophila breviligulata*, means "sand lover," is invaluable on the East coast if you have sandy land that runs down to the water, and you need to build or enlarge a dune to protect it from being washed over. With the increasing interest in protecting dunes, it is now possible to buy beach grass—the conservation committee in your town can tell you where and may even have some to sell.

If you have some dune grasses growing on your own land, they are easy to dig up and transplant. While this conflicts with what I have read elsewhere, I do not recommend that you dig up a large clump; it is hard work and may be destructive to the dune that grass is holding. Instead, take a plastic bag and sit on the beach (you might as well enjoy yourself) right at the point where the grass gives way to pure sand. Here is where you will find the youngest shoots of beach grass, not thick enough to be matted and not old enough to be connected to thick tough roots. With the aid of a trowel, gently dig in the sand around the outermost shoot and ease it out of the sand as far as you can. You will end up with a long root runner from which, at intervals, sprout individual roots and blades of grass. You can cut these up to make separate plantings of each, but it is better to wind up three or four roots and put them in one hole. If you aren't going right home to plant them, be sure to cover the plastic bag with damp sand so you don't fry the roots.

the answer. On the East Coast the first and best plant to build and save a sand dune is the native American beach grass, *Ammophila breviligulata*, which is also native to the Great Lakes. Unfortunately, its use on the Pacific coast, along with European beach grass, *Ammophila arenaria*, has virtually wiped out the native dune grass, *Leymus mollis*, and increased the height and undermined the stability of the dunes.

If you already have a dune between your house and the ocean, it's vital to protect that dune. Although beach grass is a hardy plant, with a thick brittle stalk that makes it tolerant of high salinity, direct sun, extreme heat, lack of fertile soil and even drought, it cannot survive being trampled on by people or vehicles. The passage of even one vehicle and a few people over a dune will kill a strip of grass and expose the dune to erosion. Pulling boats over a dune is a certain way to destroy it.

In the past, advice on building dunes suggested dumping old Christmas trees, tires, yard waste, car parts and other debris on the pile. Experience has shown that these are not as effective as beach grass and sand fencing; with no network of living roots to hold the dunes, storms can rip them apart and the dried trees can catch fire and destroy the dune. Building community crossovers to keep people off the dunes is another important save-the-dunes feature.

Virtually every community fronting on the water has a program to help save the dunes. Many of these have regular days when volunteers are urged to work on the community's dunes, and they also sell dune grasses to private property owners.

For excellent instructions, with clear illustrations, on how to plant and save a dune, check out the DNREC Online website article "Beachgrass Planting and Dune Preservation" found in the Bibliography in this book, or write the Delaware Department of Natural Resources and Environmental Control (DNREC), 89 Kings Highway, Dover, DE 19901.

Eroding cliffs and high banks

Picture postcards of the famous Gay Head cliffs on Martha's Vineyard show a far more colorful bank than the one that exists today. The famous red cliff has collapsed and is covered with greenery. Around the other corner of the cliff, embedded in the side of the steep embankment, is a relic of the old Coast Guard station, which was later built on a safer piece of flat land in Menemsha.

A view from Point Reyes National Monument, California.

Left: Juniper clings to steep bluffs in southern California. Corono del Mar garden. Design by Roger's Gardens Colorscape. Below: A house too close to the edge for comfort.

Along our New England shores, the sight of houses near or on a tottering bank is a reminder that the price of a glorious view may be a constant worry over the loss of land between the home and the edge of the cliff—if not worse. (This doesn't compare, of course, with the mass loss of houses from mud slides on the California coast.)

Although a remedy for this potential disaster is beyond this book, another book details in both text and extremely clear photographs how one husband and wife saved their own home. In 1960, Giorgina Reid, a textile designer and photographer, and her husband, Donald, bought a house on a high cliff facing Long Island Sound. In the hurricane of 1962, about a third of their property was washed away and their landscape was in gullies and rocks, right down to the water. To make a long story a little shorter, Giorgina came up with the idea of using the driftwood and broken reeds that were washed up on what was left of their beach. As pictured and described in her book, *How to Hold Up a Bank*, she invented what she later patented as the Reed–Trench method of terracing to control shore erosion.

Sometime later, as the Montauk Point, Long Island, lighthouse—placed 200 feet from the edge of the water in George Washington's time—had lost more than half of its land and the official attempts to hold the land with a sea wall failed time and again, Giorgina was given permission to try her method. For fifteen years, sometimes alone and sometimes with other volunteers, she built terraces between the sea wall and the lighthouse, filling in the trenches with reeds. Pictures taken twenty years after her work show that the land is stable. And the lighthouse is safe.

Although *How to Hold Up a Bank* is out of print, I would certainly recommend finding the book at your library if this is a situation that affects your own land. There is also, on the official Montauk Point Lighthouse website, a synopsis of Reid's story and process in a fascinating article by Greg Donahue: "Against All Odds: A Lighthouse Looks to the Future" (www.montauklighthouse.com/donohue.htm).

Spiraea japonica with festuca and cosmos light up a Massachusetts coastal garden. Plants with appealing garden characteristics, like the spirea, can be invasive in some regions. Dry, sandy soil may curb the plant's aggressive tendencies, but it pays to be vigilant. Epstein garden, Martha's Vineyard, Massachusetts

INVASIVE PLANTS

This is such a thorny subject that I wish I could simply omit any discussion of it in this book. In good conscience I can't, because the very attributes that make these plants desirable at the seashore—an ability to spread and take over, which also makes them hardy enough to survive in the difficult shore environment—are what so often make them invasive. That's not always the case, of course, and what's invasive in one part of the country may be fine in another. As a general rule, the invasive plant problem is going to be worse in warm climates—on the Southeast coast and California—where the weather is conducive to rapid growth and proliferation.

One of the most difficult issues for me is that too many plants are listed in one place or another as invasive. The most complete (and for me, the most irritating) reference I have is the Brooklyn Botanic Garden handbook *Invasive Plants*. It isn't that they are wrong; I don't presume to overrule their experts, but it does drive me a little crazy to find a couple of my most decorous plants listed as invasive. My pretty pink little *Spiraea japonica*, the gift of plantsman George Schenk, hasn't moved from its own small spot in thirty years. Maybe if I lived in a rich woodland beside a stream, I'd pay more attention. Tamarisk is another plant often listed as invasive, which it certainly may be in streams and wetlands, but it's a useful shrub in a sandy, salty climate.

My other confession is that I knowingly went out and bought an invasive species—Japanese barberry, *Berberis thunbergii*—which we planted in the small front yard of our apartment house in Cambridge, Massachusetts. I confess I knew it was invading the woodlands in our state when we bought it, and, okay, I feel a little guilty about that even though we live in a city and are nowhere near a woodland. (Yes, I know about birds that carry seeds.) The thing is that before the barberry, we had dogs. *All* the neighborhood dogs, whether on a leash or not. Now there isn't a single dog that despoils our pretty street garden. Recently I saw a pamphlet that suggested substitutes for invasives. But the ones for barberry wouldn't have worked at all.

At my Martha's Vineyard house I have several scented plants, including a Japanese honeysuckle, *Lonicera japonica*, growing wild next to the outdoor shower. These make taking a shower a delightfully fragrant experience. I can control the honeysuckle fairly easily and don't find it much of a problem. I can't say that about Oriental bittersweet, *Celastrus orbiculatus*. My battle to keep it from taking over the land around my

"POPULAR" INVASIVE PLANTS

On this list you'll find some of the most popular invasive plants sold (and bought) at garden centers today. Some are problems in certain coastal areas; some are widely invasive, but a plant named here should send a red flag in your direction.

ailanthus, *Ailanthus altissima*

Australian pine, *Casuarina*

autumn olive, *Elaeagnus umbellata*

burning bush, *Euonymus alatus*

Chinese privet, *Ligustrum sinense*

crown vetch, *Coronilla*

English ivy, *Hedera helix*

eucalyptus, *Eucalyptus globulus*

goutweed, *Aegopodium podagraria*

ice plant, *Carpobrotus chilensis*

Japanese barberry, *Berberis thunbergii*

Japanese honeysuckle, *Lonicera japonica*

Norway maple, *Acer platanoides*

oriental bittersweet, *Celastrus orbiculatus*

pampas grass, *Cortaderia selloana*

princess tree, *Paulownia tomentosa*

purple loosestrife, *Lythrum salicaria*

Russian olive, *Elaeagnus angustifolia*

Scotch broom, *Cytisus scoparius*

sycamore maple, *Acer pseudoplatanus*

English ivy, *Hedera helix*

Scotch broom, *Cytisus scoparius*, grows among rocks along the Oregon coast.

house has been ongoing for more than thirty years. I don't expect to win it. But if I ever gave up the fight, that's all that would be growing here.

Two trees that I can't tell apart are *Elaeagnus umbellata*, autumn olive, and *Elaeagnus angustifolia*, Russian olive. Like so many plants that have become invasive, these two were originally encouraged because they could survive, even thrive, in the harsh environments of the shore, or because they could solve a problem such as erosion control.

From the point of view of the gardener, these olives are very much alike. Autumn olive, more shrublike, is invasive along the East Coast but Russian olive is not. In the Midwest, Russian olive, a small tree, has escaped cultivation and is highly invasive, but autumn olive is not. Or so the experts say; I could swear the trees I see attempting to take over Martha's Vineyard are Russian olives, which aren't supposed to be invasive here.

They are also hard to eradicate because in many ways they are ideal shorefront plants. Unfazed by wind or salt, able to grow in sand because of their nitrogen-fixing root nodules, and attractive in a seaworthy way, these trees take a stronger will than mine to be gotten rid of. I do remove a few every year, in the hope that I can keep them from taking over the neighborhood. If you can find it, *Elaeagnus commutata* is a prettier American relative whose running roots help to stabilize banks and sandy soil.

The better the growing climate, the more difficult the problems with invasive plants. We have already considered *Ammophila breviligulata*, imported to help erosion, which has overwhelmed the native West Coast grasses and created unstable high dunes there. Other plants that were originally imported to stabilize dunes and protect the shores against erosion now flourish unbounded on those dunes and exacerbate the problem. Judith Larner Lowry, the California native plant landscaper, says that in the coastal gardens she works with, most of the time and money goes to eradicating these plants: German ivy, *Delairea odorata*; English ivy, *Hedera helix*; ice plant, *Carpobrotus chilensis*; and capeweed, *Arctotheca calendula*. In addition, the California Exotic Pest Plant Council recommends avoiding these species that thrive only too well on the California coast: Scotch broom, *Cytisus scoparius*; pampas grass, *Cortaderia jubata*; and blue gum eucalyptus, *Eucalyptus globulus*.

Unfortunately, every one of these plants is carried in nurseries and garden centers, so the fact that they are being sold does not mean that they are safe. My advice, finally, is to check the list of invasives in this and other books, and don't buy those plants. And the Brooklyn Botanic Garden book is certainly a good place to start. But be sure to read the fine print to see where and under what circumstances the plant is invasive. If the plant is already growing in your garden, let your environmental conscience be your guide.

NATIVES ONLY?

I wrote my first gardening book, *Gardening with Wildflowers*, as a consequence of building a house on Martha's Vineyard and starting, in all innocence, to make a garden on this sandy, duney, acre and a half of land overlooking a beautiful water view. Until then, my only experience had been in a heavily shaded suburban garden.

Since I had written about wildflowers I felt constrained to use only native plants in my new seashore garden—and only those that were native to this particular spot. Actually, I was both ignorant and insufferably pure about it, and for several years, I didn't improve the "soil" or plant anything that wasn't growing on our land before we arrived.

Well, you can get pretty tired of a garden limited to beach plum, bayberry, beach rose, and even an occasional blue-eyed grass. Only poison ivy was not welcomed. When the hardcover edition of my book went out of print, I threw off my self-imposed restrictions and had a great time buying any plant that appealed to me—even though I made all the mistakes I hope this book will help you avoid.

This is a very longwinded way of bringing up the issue of whether you should grow only native species in your garden. In general, you certainly will be more successful if you do. And I cannot help but admire conservationist gardeners whose intent is to try to restore our native flora. Throughout the plant directory, I've indicated those that are native, and I've usually said where in the United States they come from.

Which brings up the question is how pure you want to be. One of my most knowledgeable authors is William Cullina, the propagator and nursery manager for the New England Wild Flower Society. Since the society, even though it carries the New England name, considers its purview to be native plants of the United States, that's good enough for me. Whatever you decide to do is up to you, and as long as you don't deliberately introduce invasive or destructive plants, I urge you not to feel guilty or defensive (or self-righteous) and nothing but joyful at achieving success at this most interesting branch of practical horticulture.

A given of seaside gardening is sandy soil that may have little or no organic content.
Fruchtman garden, Stinson Beach, California

GARDENS AT THE SHORE

A Puget Sound home looks onto a lush garden on one side and the wild, rocky harbor on the other. *Sedum* 'Autumn Joy', *Malus* 'Spartan', *Calluna*, and *Erica carnea* 'Springwood White' bloom amidst conifers. Design by Steve Schramm and Richard Haag

Over the years I have learned, by trial and many errors, how to garden by the sea. And in this section I have the pleasure of showing you pictures of some gardens that have faced and survived various degrees of coastal weather. I think you'll enjoy the visit, and I'm sure you'll get some good ideas that you can transplant to your own garden.

As I look back on my own years of gardening at the shore, I realize that until I started writing this book, I didn't personally know anyone else who was doing this variation on "regular" gardening. As the gardening editor at Houghton Mifflin, I edited the *Taylor's Guide to Seashore Gardening*, but this was primarily the work of other writers. I saw their pictures of coast gardens and of plants that would grow there, and I read what they said, but I still hadn't visited any gardens that had the mark (and the heady smell) of the Atlantic Ocean about them. Until I edited that book, everything I had learned about gardening came from lectures, books, many of which I edited, and above all from my gardening mother. None of this was specific to land near the water. One year a local magazine asked me to write about the influence of my job on my garden, and I remember describing my modest small landscape and saying that I would never invite one of my authors to visit. When the article appeared it was illustrated with a gorgeous picture of somebody else's spectacular seashore garden and I had to fend off readers' requests to visit.

PACIFIC NORTHWEST

Two San Juan Island gardens

San Juan Island is the largest of the 170 San Juan Islands in Puget Sound. In the first of the gardens we visit here, landscape designer Steve Schramm explained his choice of grasses as accomplishing a number of blessings. Dwarf selections of *Miscanthus sinensis* connect the house to the surrounding meadows while at the same time adding a softening effect. The grasses also stand up well against the winds, which, depending on the time of year, blast the garden from three different directions.

The hope of blending the grasses with plants native to the area didn't work out though. Voracious deer around the property feasted on salal, Oregon grape, and *Ceanothus*—the very plants they ignored elsewhere. Over time, some of those plants survived, thanks to a nonstop deer repellant spray program.

One challenge at the shore is choosing plants to fit the climate. Another is how to connect with the existing, often beautiful, shoreline

Calluna and *Erica* cultivars in a bed bordered by *Miscanthus sinensis.*
Design by Steve Schramm

Miscanthus sinensis 'Yaku-jima', other *Miscanthus*, and *Gaultheria shallon* grow on the protected side of this Juan Island house, out of the way of direct winds. Design by Steve Schramm

A flagstone path between plantings of *Miscanthus sinensis* in their fall color. Design by Steve Schramm

edge. Schramm says, "I like to mimic what I see along the native, natural edge of San Juan Island; this translates into using the same plants found at the edge or look-alikes. I like to repeat or echo rock and vegetation patterns, colors, and textures while still paying attention to climate adaptability.

"I also find it useful and aesthetically pleasing to create some contrast with the edge. This contrast can be through color or texture or by using vertical elements that provide foreground for views, as well as the potential for modifying the climate. This can create a protected and sheltered feeling, and opportunities for expanding the plant palate."

———————

For twenty years Schramm and his colleagues worked with the owner of a ten-acre San Juan Island property to make it increasingly livable without sacrificing its natural drama. Each room in the house is linked to the outdoor pathways; as much thought was given to framing window views from inside the house as to the outdoor experience of the same spaces.

The entry through a mossy forest of blooming trees—stewartia, amelanchier, and kousa dogwood—gives no hint of the raw and wild rocky bluff that awaits at the western edge. From the whale-watch deck, cantilevered over the steep cliff, there is a close view of the dolphins, seals, and orca whales swimming in the deep water below. One of the many paths leads from the barbecue area, past the sculpture garden, to the vegetable garden nestled between two rock outcrops. The sculpture, *Whale Tails*, is by Peter Busby.

The steep path leading to the whale-watch deck is lined with low-growing *Arbutus unedo* and a variety of heaths and heathers. Design by Steve Schramm and Richard Haag

Amidst deep-hued ceanothus, from the stone barbecue past the *Whale Tails* sculpture garden, the path leads to a dining deck and the vegetable garden where tomatoes are ripening. Design by Steve Schramm and Richard Haag

CALIFORNIA

TERRY CAMICCIA'S GARDEN

Terry Camiccia and her husband, Ralph, live on a cliff at the ocean's edge in Bolinas, a small rural town in Marin County at the southern-most tip of the Point Reyes National Seashore. The worst storms arrive from November to February, but her place is always windy. "On the north side of the house, it's like living in a wind tunnel." On the plus side, she looks directly across the bay to San Francisco.

The constant winds in Terry Camiccia's garden keep her bamboo at thirty feet high, but storms often shred the top foliage. She prunes up the trunks of her bamboo "forest" as far as she can to see the legs move in the wind. When the bamboo spreads beyond where she wants it, she simply cuts the wandering stem to the ground.

Her impressive Japanese timber bamboo began as a slip from her grandfather thirty years ago. Terry learned all her gardening skills from that same grandfather, in particular the way to prune plants and fruit trees tightly, so they don't blow over in the wind. "Over the years, I've learned to take out all the plants that don't do well in wind and fog. And from my travels to Japan and Italy, I've learned to love topiary. I'm having fun keeping my shrubs pruned tight and making shapes."

Roses and bamboo flank a gate behind the house and out of the wind.
Camiccia garden, Bolinas, California

This impressive bamboo, with *Hebe* growing beneath in Terry Camiccia's California garden, is the Japanese timber bamboo *Phyllostachys bambusoides*.

Among the topiaries are *Hebe*, *Picea abies*, *Buxus* and many other foliage plants, which protect a seating area from the wind. Camiccia garden, Bolinas, California

Roses, hydrangeas, and deutzia on the protected side of Terry's garden.

SALLY ROBERTSON'S GARDEN

Sally Robertson lives near Terry Camiccia in Bolinas. "The natural beauty is stunning, so it is especially challenging to us gardeners to compete with that," Sally notes. Two facts make her garden the showplace that it is. Although she lives on a mesa where constant wind is the norm, her land is in a dip in the terrain, and wind passes harmlessly over it. The other distinguishing feature is that Sally is a noted painter of flowers. Her garden is filled with the flowers that are the subjects she paints.

One plant Robertson could happily live without are the Monterey cypresses she inherited from the previous owners of her house. "I consider [cypresses] coastal weeds, and would never plant them, but I did inherit many when I bought my property twenty-six years ago. I had to remove the ones that were becoming dangerous and unsightly. We do not have the same winds that shape them so beautifully farther south in Monterey County, and here they grow to great and uncontrolled heights.

The flowers that are the subject of their gardener's paintings pose beside the house. Robertson garden, Bolinas, California

Imaginatively pruned
Monterey cypress. Robertson
garden, Bolinas, California

"The cypresses along the street side of the garden had been roughly trained as a hedge, and I tried to maintain that idea for the first few years. But as dead tree material built up on the inside, and they became less than pleasing, I decided to try something different. Over ten years or so, we took out about one third of the trees every year, gradually bonsaiing the remaining ones, with the help of local tree men—I don't do chainsaw work myself!

"Now we only have to go in and reshape the 'clouds' with electric clippers and tall ladders once yearly. These trees are the most expensive and high-maintenance part of my garden, and I would never advise planting them."

Sally's newest garden inspiration for her art is a pond she had installed where she can grow water lilies and other water-loving plants.

A pond with waterlilies, and nasturtiums and irises in the background.

NORTHEAST

Nan Sinton's garden

Nan Sinton is one of those people who seems able to conduct several lives at one time. She may be best known to gardeners who read *Horticulture* for the many national and international garden tours she leads each year. She is, in addition, a landscape designer who has lived and gardened in the brunt of the worst winds that hit the Boston area seashore.

The sea view from her Hingham property was breathtaking, she says—180 degrees of ocean bay, with the buildings of downtown Boston rising to the west.

But this incredible view did not hide the site's challenges: wild northeast winter winds, branch-breaking ice storms, and moon tide waves that sprayed saltwater far into the garden. Storm damage convinced Sinton that the first thing she had to do was protect the garden, which she did with a combination of living plants and constructed forms. Her eight-foot-tall wind baffle fence is made of sturdy 1 × 4 boards, spaced about one and a half inches apart (to let some wind blow through) and inset with panels of lattice, which in spring and summer are dressed with vines. Eventually she added stone walls as well.

Sinton also created a living windbreak, a hedge of wild *Rosa rugosa*, which she planted from slips and pruned to the ground each year. Among the roses, she also planted privet, willow, autumn olive, and black locust trees.

On a clear summer day, the view across the water to Boston in the distance shows no sign of the power of winter storms. Nan Sinton's *Rosa rugosa* hedge provides a natural windbreak. Photos by Nan Sinton

The view out the window at the icy shore.

After a series of storms, stone seemed the only answer. It was time to replace rickety structures with some solid granite walls.

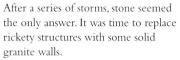

Sinton's design for an attractive and practical wooden storm fence.

A birdhouse stands among naturalized roses and other plants in the open land between the property and the shore.
Design by Phyllis McMorrow

NORTH SHORE GARDEN

A magnificent property on a high piece of land overlooking Vineyard Sound is open to the harsh elements of the New England seashore. The windy open land in front of the house was certainly not conducive to a garden, and designer Phyllis McMorrow had to plant her beautiful gardens elsewhere.

In the marginal protection of some trees and the house itself, the blue and white border is composed primarily of catmints, perennial salvias, and native daisies, all hardy enough to stand up to the wind.

This still left no place for a garden protected from wind and comfortable to sit in and read the paper over breakfast. For that the owner had local stone mason Lew French create a fanciful stone-and-wood enclosure with a door kept firmly closed to keep the turtles in and the deer out.

Luxuriant and colorful flowers grow inside the enclosed garden. Among the stars are *Thymus ×citriodorus* 'Aureus', *Artemisia stelleriana* 'Silver Brocade', and *Campanula* 'Kent Belle'.

A long border of *Salvia* ×*sylvestris* 'Mainacht', *Nepeta* 'Walker's Low', *Leucanthemum vulgare*, and *Belamcanda* foliage is barely protected by trees.

The inner garden, which includes *Veronicastrum virginicum* 'Fascination' and *Astilbe japonica* 'Deutschland' among other plantings, is protected by stone walls connected to the house.

Delphinium and *Clematis* 'Paul Farges' flourish inside the garden walls.

A fence protects a border of roses, *Oenothera*, *Eupatorium*, and *Chrysanthemum* on this windswept Martha's Vineyard property. Taylor garden

TRUDY TAYLOR'S GARDEN

Only a narrow strip of stony sand—Stonewall Beach—separates Trudy Taylor's land from the Atlantic Ocean. Two groups of Japanese black pines stand like sentinels against the winds off the sea, but a natural hedge of *Rosa rugosa* and wild grape vines actually protects the sitting area.

With the additional protection of a fence, Trudy's Chilmark garden includes Joe Pye weed and evening primrose and even *Delphinium*, which she grows as an annual, and the tall yellow meadow rue, *Thalictrum flavum*.

Within her cozy plant-filled house (where son James Taylor's gold and platinum records fill one wall) an attached greenhouse is home to singing finches, tree frogs, and chameleons among the trees and vines. Out in back is the compost bin that supplies the garden with rich black loam.

A peaceful seating area in the garden with a hedge of *Rosa rugosa* and wild grape nearby.

Wind-blown delphinium, allium, *Thalictrum flavum*, and *Veronica*.

The attached greenhouse and hardworking compost bin in the backyard.

Liriope, *Perovskia*, and *Achillea* on either side of the path around the garden, with the natural wild landscape beyond. Feldman garden. Design by Wolfgang Oehme

GRETCHEN AND SAM FELDMAN'S GARDEN

Gretchen and Sam Feldman's Martha's Vineyard land overlooks a branch of Chilmark Pond, one of the Great Ponds along the Atlantic Ocean shore of the island. The land is comprised of soft rounded meadows of Joe Pye weed and native grasses.

When they bought the land, the Feldmans' goal was to blend their house into the natural landscape, not to protect themselves from the elements that shaped it.

This led them to hire Wolfgang Oehme, of Oehme, van Sweden & Associates, known for their "New American Garden" style of landscape design. This metaphor for the American meadow reflects the year-round beauty of the natural landscape. In the Feldmans' garden, large ornamental grasses and colorful sweeps of perennials, like Japanese iris, anemones, Russian sage, and *Gaura lindheimeri*, provide color all season long from June until frost. The flowers are protected in some cases by the house, but predominantly by the large clumps of ornamental grasses.

Although their garden blends in seamlessly with the surrounding meadow, the Feldmans are careful not to let their nursery plants stray into the wild landscape. I watched Gretchen Feldman, with her artist's eye, locate the tiniest weed in her beds and could see that an unwanted plant didn't have a chance.

Salvia ×sylvestris growing among grasses and other plantings.

Large clumps of ornamental grasses protect *Penstemon digitalis* 'Husker's Red', *Iris ensata*, and other grasses.

The house protects perennials from the wind.

The path that painter Robert Dash called his "view snatcher" was eight feet wide at the start and six feet where his land ended, exaggerating the distance. Eventually new construction snatched the view. Dash garden

ROBERT DASH'S GARDEN

If artist Robert Dash built a landscape on the edge of a glacier, I'm sure it would be worth seeing. As luck would have it, though, his humorous, enchanting, and horticulturally impressive garden, Madoo, is located in the town of Sagaponack at the eastern end of Long Island in New York. Furthermore, since Madoo has been opened as a public conservancy, you actually can visit it.

What makes Madoo such a remarkable garden is not only Dash's artistry and his sense of humor, but his dirt gardener's knowledge of what it takes to make things grow. These are the things you don't see—like the five truckloads of manure that are brought in every year. Or the pruning shears that are always in his hand when he walks through Madoo.

The first time I visited Madoo, I was enchanted by the view, which reached from the end of his land to the ocean beyond it. By the time I visited in 2004, the view had disappeared behind a landscape of Mc-Mansions. The brick path was still there, but Dash had erected at the end of it an "exedra," a stone edifice half round at the top, which he described as a fifth century demilune, a garden spot where the Greeks used to sit to tell secrets to the gods. To make it easier to communicate with the gods, he put an obelisk at the top.

Still not satisfied, Dash built a long narrow rill of water down the middle of the path, mimicking the dimensions of the path by making the rill eight inches at the beginning and six inches at the end, where it meets the exedra. Then he inserted a matching length of mirror up the face of the exedra. Now when you look down the path, what you apparently see is a long rill of water at the end of which is a beautiful landscape. Of course what you are really seeing is the part of Dash's own garden that's behind you, reflected in the mirror.

Many other delights you will see at Madoo are pictured on these pages.

The ginkgo trees and the boxwood balls. You won't be far off if these remind you of Alice in Wonderland playing croquet with the hedgehogs as the balls.

Laburnum is notoriously intolerant of salt-laden winds from the sea, but with strong posts to support them, wind-breaking trellises, and charming gaiters of ivy to clothe their dull trunks and protect them against the salt, the *Laburnum* arbor is a highlight of this two-acre garden.

The curved shingled roof of the Asian bridge (The Bridge of the Bankrupt Painter) prevents witches, goblins, imps, and other riff-raff from jumping off and attacking you. Instead, they slide off, screaming imprecations as they go. Dash garden

SOUTHEAST

SOUTH COAST GARDEN

Kiawah is noted for several things: its long sand beach, its championship golf courses, and its gated communities. Although it sells itself as a resort, it also has year-round houses with one door on the street (or marshy side) and the other facing the Atlantic Ocean and the beach. The owner of this house, an antique dealer who makes many trips to the France she loves, wanted the look and feel of Normandy for her house and garden.

Ligustrum japonicum shades a decorative bench and a planting of rosemary at its feet.
Dixon garden. Design by Bill Maneri

The wind and the local environmental officers decree that nothing be planted in the sand on the water side. Instead petunia cultivars and young palms make a colorful corner on a deck in their antique wine barrels.
Dixon garden. Design by Bill Maneri

From the back door of the house, the wooden boardwalk leads safely over the dunes to the beach. Dixon garden. Design by Bill Maneri; architect Christopher Rose

Sabal palmettos line the walk on the street side of the house.

ADVICE FROM SEASHORE GARDENERS

Clematis don't spring to mind as candidates for seaside gardens, but given sufficient
water and partial shade in the hottest part of the day, they, too, will thrive.

"The sun is so powerful here, it burns a lot of flowers that say full sun on their packages. Now if it says full sun, I plant in partial sun, and so forth. I always give my plants twice the recommended amount of water, and never during the day when the water will burn holes in the leaves."

—a Georgia gardener living two miles from the ocean

When all is said and done, there is nothing like the direct experience of knowledgeable people who have worked in a specific region. Here, mostly in their own words, is what some of the experts who have been most helpful to me have to say.

CADY GOLDFIELD

Cady Goldfield, a garden designer who lives and works on the north shore of Massachusetts, grew up in Marblehead, literally on the water. Her family's home was on top of a fifty-foot seawall and embankment and the view from her bedroom window was the Atlantic Ocean. She spent her teen years gardening in the back, from the porch to the edge of the embankment. There was full sun all day and often wind. The plants that grew best were the naturally rugged ones: tansy, goldenrod, beach plum, Queen Anne's lace, and *Rosa rugosa*.

Many of her clients live near the water, and she has had success with plants that do well in an alpine environment, those with thick, waxy, leathery foliage and a streamlined shape that allows the wind to slip over it. Conversely, she also likes plants with supple leaves, like the grasses and bamboos she specializes in.

Cady also advises using rocks and boulders as planting shelters, following the same principles you would follow for making a rock garden.

Tough customers such as California poppies (*Eschscholzia californica*) and lamb's ears (*Stachys byzantina*) can be expected to revel in seaside conditions.

The rocks are used to deflect the wind and absorb radiation, which will be released as heat well into the night. Where you place the rocks depends on the terrain, the sun exposure, and the direction of the prevailing winds; if the barrier is on a slope or at the base of a hill, the wind can create a cold cell. Boulders work best if they are low lying, smooth, rounded forms, not vertical craggy ones. They must be placed so that the wind passing over them will not hit a planting bed. The effect for the plant on the leeward side of the rock should be that of a protective cave which the wind passes over harmlessly and the sun warms.

GRASSES FOR LANDSCAPES

Here is Cady Goldfield's advice about grasses she has grown successfully near or on the coast.

Ammophila breviligulata (beach grass or marram grass)

This is about the most salt-wind-and-sand–tolerant grass you can plant by the shore. It will grow in sand, making it ideal for beachfront cottages tucked into the dunes. A native of the East Coast and the Michigan dunes on the Great Lakes, this species, which grows about 24 inches high, is hardy in USDA zones 5 to 9. Gardeners would be doing a good deed by planting beach grass (purchased from native-plant nurseries), as it's endangered and also is a valuable tool for holding together unstable dunes.

Chasmanthium latifolium (northern sea oats)

One of my favorites for its sensory charms. It has nodding seed heads that rustle in the breeze, providing winter interest. It can handle coastal winds by bending like bamboo then recovering its upright form during calm spells. Northern sea oats will form a colony if you let it, and in my experience it readily self-seeds (I've had it pop up in unexpected places in my garden). It's not hard to keep it in bounds, but it's really best, I've found, for planting in masses. This also accentuates the wonderful sound effects when the dry foliage and seed heads are stirred by autumn and winter winds. It will grow 24 inches to 36 inches high (stems for the flower and seed heads can get to 4 feet) and is reliably hardy in zones 5 to 9.

Festuca glauca 'Elijah Blue' (blue fescue 'Elijah Blue')

This blue-gray fescue grows in mounds that get 6 inches tall, with seed heads that can reach 12 inches or taller. It is evergreen in sheltered spots, but will probably die to the ground in very windy, cold areas although the dried foliage can be attractive and also doesn't disintegrate by late winter the way some grasses do. It will get leggy and lose its neat habit in shade or part shade, so I recommend planting it in full sun.

Helictotrichon sempervirens (blue oat grass)

Hardy in zones 4 to 9, this is a striking blue-gray, spiky grass that is a good substitute for *Festuca glauca* and in fact is more durable. It forms mounds up to 36 inches wide and about 18 inches tall, though the

Festuca glauca 'Elijah Blue'

Miscanthus sinensis 'Yaku-jima'

Panicum virgatum 'Heavy Metal'

Chasmanthium latifolium

Helictotrichon sempervirens

Panicum virgatum 'Warrior'

Pennisetum alopecuroides

flowering stems and heads can reach 24 inches or more in height. It can endure strong coastal winds and tolerates poor soils as long as they're well drained.

Miscanthus sinensis 'Yaku-jima' (dwarf silver grass)

This is a dwarf *Miscanthus* that forms mounds about 4 feet tall (6 feet with plumes) and is hardy in zones 6 to 9. *Miscanthus* is tolerant of salt spray, making it ideal for coastal landscapes. The smaller size of "Yaku-jima" makes it easier to maintain than many of the larger *Miscanthus* varieties. Because *Miscanthus* has a tendency to disintegrate in late winter, I suggest using the more compact cultivars that do not make such a big mess. While the foliage is living, it is very durable and withstands coastal winds well. The foliage undulates in the wind, creating a striking effect. This is a warm-season grass, so I recommend planting it in the sunniest spots where the ground warms early in spring. Otherwise, it may not return until June in the cooler end of its hardiness zone.

Panicum virgatum (switch grass)

I like switch grass for its versatility—it tolerates a broad range of soil conditions from dry and sandy to swampy (I have one that grows in my fish pond with its roots completely underwater). It has an upright form, with flowers that are pinkish and ethereal-looking panicles; they look lovely when rippling in a breeze. I've found switch grass to be very tolerant of wind, and the dried foliage and seed heads hold up well throughout winter in a challenging location like the seacoast. Plant it in a sunny spot, and it will thrive for a long time. This native grass is hardy from zones 5 to 9 and grows 3 feet tall (6 feet with its long flower or seed stalks).

Pennisetum alopecuroides (fountain grass)

The more compact cultivars seem to do well by the seaside. The fuzzy seed heads stay intact in all but gale-force winds, and the dry foliage maintains its form through the winter. 'Little Bunny' is a good edging plant, as its small mounds are low-slung (making them wind resistant), tidy and well behaved. 'Hameln' forms 20-to-30-inch mounds and is good for massing or as a specimen planting. *Pennisetum* is slightly tolerant of salt spray, but should be planted in locations where it won't be constantly exposed to spray.

Pseudosasa japonica (arrow bamboo)

This is a bamboo—which is a member of the grass family—that is tolerant of salt spray and winds, making it an excellent choice for coastal embankments and other spots where a durable, spreading grass is needed for erosion control, screening, and good looks. It thrives in zones 7 to 9 but will also survive in zone 6, though it will die back to the ground and return in spring like a perennial if winter temperatures dip below 0 degrees F. In milder climates, it can grow 18 inches tall and form small groves; in cooler zones it may reach a height of 6 inches. As this plant spreads by rhizomes, I recommend planting within natural barriers such as between a ledge and the ocean; otherwise, use a containment method such as a trench, annual mowing of errant shoots, or an underground metal or plastic border.

ANN HUNT

Back when I first knew her, a long time ago, Hunt owned a nursery on Martha's Vineyard. Although I didn't realize it at the time, those small Japanese black pines we dug up from her fields were my first exploration into seashore gardening. When I got in touch with her about this book, Hunt had since retired to the Lowcountry of South Carolina, settling near the coast south of Charleston.

"Here the living is easy," she told me, "and gardening in heat and humidity is a real challenge. It has taken me twelve years of mistakes to figure it out, between swatting marsh mosquitoes and avoiding fire ants. I hope some of these suggestions will help you avoid some of my mistakes.

"Seashore gardening around the world is site specific. Each site has its own wind, soil, and related maritime conditions that must be understood and dealt with on an individual basis. One solution does not fit all. Rather, you need to use common sense coupled with time spent studying the site to be landscaped. The best time to study a site is during a storm. Then you can walk a property with rain and wind stinging your face, looking for those natural quiet spots, which the land topography may provide.

"It is impossible to control wind. But it is possible to study the nature of prevailing winds and create fences, stone walls, or hedgerows to baffle the wind and create quiet microclimes on the lee side.

"During a nor'easter or any big blow, walk along the perimeter of your house with your back to the building. You may find a quiet spot that could make a good microclimate for a garden, or even a place to grow a special tree or shrub.

"To mark the direction of the wind, stake out balloons on a windy site and study their pitch and yaw.

"Plant salt-tolerant plants. After a storm hose down your plants to remove salt.

"Perhaps one of the most misunderstood seashore gardening problems is how to deal with sandy, clay, or rocky soils. The best method is to amend the soil at the surface and not try to dig nourishment into the soil. It is a case of adding layer upon layer of compost and mulch through the years and letting it leach down into the depth of plant roots. This is especially true of sand and clay soils. Sometimes the answer may be to build raised beds filled with good topsoil and amendments. And for those fortunate enough to have seaweed floating in on the tide, collect it, hose it down to remove salts, and compost it.

FIND A FRIEND AT GARDENWEB

One piece of good advice is to ask your neighboring gardeners what works or doesn't work for them. Here are some neighbors you probably didn't think you had. They are living at **www.GardenWeb .com/forums/regional**.

GardenWeb is a large computer site composed of about a hundred different "forums" divided by kind of plants, gardening subjects, and regions. Within those forums, members ask questions and other members answer them. Anyone can be a member.

For seashore gardeners like us, the best forums are the regional ones.

I, for instance, just went to New England, and from there I narrowed my search to the Northeast coast. On that site I found a member who asked about salt-tolerant shrubs. One answer came from a member I recognized from a year ago. He offered an excellent list. Whether you have a question or simply are interested in what other gardeners in your region have to say, gardenweb. com is an intriguing place to visit. A question that aroused great interest had to do with using crushed seashells in the garden. To judge from the number of replies, a lot of seashore gardeners are interested in that subject.

"To the novice just beginning to garden directly by the sea, spend time understanding the wind patterns on your site. Understand that you will make mistakes. Understand that planting small-sized shrubs and trees allowing them to adjust to adverse conditions is a good idea.

"Maritime gardening is a challenge in some locations. Feel the wind. Understand the conditions. Relish the challenge."

DORIE ECKARD REDMON

> **FACTORS TO CONSIDER WHEN CHOOSING PLANTS**
>
> • tolerance to salt in the air and sodium in the soil
>
> • tolerance to heat and drought
>
> • attractiveness to deer
>
> The ever-increasing pressure from hungry deer narrows our plant options. Try using herbs and other plants with strong aromas in your ornamental garden.

Redmon is a garden designer and consultant to property owners and businesses in the Lowcountry, an area between Charleston, South Carolina, and Savannah, Georgia. "Much of the area," she writes, "is still dedicated to truck farming, mostly tomatoes. The barrier islands, those small landforms that are actually located within Atlantic Ocean waters, seem to be taken up by (literally) hundreds of golf courses and resort developments. I've done work in both types of environments.

"Coastal gardening can be quite a challenge. We don't think of our treasured seaside property as a hostile environment, but our plants might—constant winds that are laden with salt, soils that are naturally salty, occasional saltwater intrusion into the ground water, and hot summer sunshine.

"If you are a novice gardener, the worst thing you can do is visit a big box store and load up your cart with plants that appeal to you. Visit a local garden center and look at the plants growing in your area.

"If you live near saltwater," Dorie concludes, "here's a trick I learned from golf courses along the coast. Excess sodium causes havoc in our soils, causing them to lose their structure and have poor water infiltration and air movement. Sodium can be removed from soil by adding gypsum in combination with *deep, infrequent* watering. Gypsum replaces the sodium ions with calcium ions, allowing the sodium to be leached through the soil out of reach of the plant roots. Gypsum does not alter the soil pH and can be applied several times a year if necessary. Buy granulated gypsum (the powdered formulation makes a real mess) and apply it at the rate of about 40 to 60 pounds per thousand square feet. A once-a-year application in the fall would go a long way toward restoring and maintaining soil health. And healthy thriving plants are dependent on that great soil!"

GEORGE GUTHRIE

George Guthrie is the landscape maintenance superintendent at Shore Acres State Park overlooking the Pacific Ocean south of Coos Bay, Oregon. He points out that there are some significant differences between gardening on the West Coast (cool dry summer and wet comparatively mild winter) and gardening at the corresponding latitude on the East Coast (wet summer and potentially colder winter). For the Pacific Northwest gardener who is just starting out, he suggests:

Plant small. Large plants are liable to blow over or rock in the wind, and may not establish well.

Plant in the fall or earliest winter. Cool moist temperatures allow the plants to get established before the dry season arrives in late May or so.

Mulch heavily around new plants to help conserve moisture in thin or sandy soils.

Choose plants that are drought- and wind-tolerant as well as accepting of low nutrient levels in the soil. In addition to certain native species, that means Mediterranean plants— rosemary, *Santolina*, lavender, sages, South Africans—*Kniphofia*, *Agapanthus*, *Watsonia*; and certain southern hemisphere plants like *Phormium*, New Zealand flax, and *Escallonia*. All of these recommendations are for gardens in the most exposed coastal areas.

Guthrie continues, "Inland a little, the selection of plants is tremendous, the growing season is long, and as long as plants and gardeners can tolerate comparatively low heat, and fog in the summer and wind and rain in the winter, they can create beautiful year-round gardens. A friend who lives less than half a mile from the beach has created a wonderful garden of heaths and heathers on almost pure sand dunes using old strips of carpet as a mulch to conserve moisture, suppress weeds, and help keep the sand stable around his new 'baby' plants. Talk about extreme gardening!"

SOME CONIFERS FOR SEASHORE GARDENS

Chamaecyparis lawsoniana
Cryptomeria japonica
Cupressus macrocarpa
Juniperus
Picea glauca
Picea mariana
Pinus contorta
Pinus thunbergii (shown below)

BROADLEAF EVERGREENS

Acacia cultriformis
Arbutus menziesii
Arctostaphylos
Calluna
Gaultheria shallon
Heteromeles salicifolia
Ilex
Myrica californica
Myrica cerifera
Nerium oleander
palms
Pyracantha
Quercus virginiana

PICK THEM BY
THEIR PETALS

Rosarian Peter Schneider offers this help for gardeners who want roses—other than *R. rugosa*—at the shore. Seacoasts are notoriously sunny, sandy, and windy, and home to heavy fog and dew. Each of these factors affects roses in a different way.

- Intense sunlight makes many yellow and apricot roses look dirty white, a particular problem with some of David Austin's roses, bred in overcast England.

- Sandy soil needs enrichment for all roses but *R. rugosa*.

- Wind tells you to grow bushy roses, not the tall thin hybrid teas and grandifloras that will be rocked and have their roots loosened in its gusts.

- Fog and dew warns against the old garden roses with lots of petals, a special problem on the West Coast. They may never open before the buds rot and drop off.

- 'Betty Prior' is a beautiful delicate-looking but tough single-petal rose that is perfectly adapted to the seashore.

VALERIE EASTON

Easton, a garden columnist for the *Seattle Times* and regional columnist for *Horticulture*, gardens on Whidbey Island north of Seattle. I interviewed her about gardening on the Pacific Northwest coast.

"Cannon Beach in Oregon is one of my favorite seaside towns. Public trails run between the houses and the beach so you can enjoy the crash of the surf on one side while you catch tantalizing glimpses of luscious gardens on the other. Weathered gray shingle cottages serve as backdrops to extravagant perennial gardens, or more naturalistic sweeps of tough grasses and windblown pines.

"How can you make such glorious gardens when the plants are exposed to burning salt spray, intense sunlight, and gale-force winds? The answer lies in choosing plants that tolerate these conditions, as well as using hedging as windbreaks to protect less sturdy plants. You can have your begonias, tea roses, dainty corydalis, and bleeding hearts if you plant a few yews, pines, and rugosa roses between them and the worst of the weather.

"But I've discovered that it's often not the plants I'd expect that survive and even thrive in blazing sun, gale force winds, and salty sea spray. Here are a few I've seen growing and blooming happily in exposed seaside conditions in the San Juan Islands:

Lavatera

lavender

wallflowers

the red-bladed ornamental grass *Panicum virgatum*,
    also *Miscanthus* and blue fescue

Rosa 'The Fairy' and *R.* 'Bonica'

"One key to finding the right plants for any condition is paying attention to what has thrived in the area for decades, whether native or introduced plants. Big old clumps of peonies can still be found blooming around early settlers' cabins in the San Juan Islands, proving that despite their delicate looks, peonies are tough survivors."

JUDITH LARNER LOWRY

Lowry is the proprietor of Larner Seeds, a mail order company specializing in California native seeds and plants. She also designs and installs native-plant gardens in the San Francisco Bay area.

Writing in *Taylor's Guide to Seashore Gardening*, she says; "The precipitous unstable coastal bluffs of California offer spectacular views and not always deep sleep at night for the homeowners perched on them. Surface erosion, slumps, and landslides are a part of life. Irrigated lawns or plantings that require regular water are to be avoided anywhere near coastal cliffs . . . A group of tough, tenacious, drought-tolerant, deep-rooted, floriferous, and easy-to-grow perennials and subshrubs help hold the California sea bluffs."

Lowry suggests: "Low-growing forms of coyote bush and California sagebrush mixed with beach aster, *Erigeron glaucus*; sea pink, *Armeria maritima*; California poppy; Bolinas lupine and other native lupines; chalk buckwheat (an important butterfly food and source of nectar); and several small native sedums.

Erigerons, bamboo, and hydrangeas line an inviting path. Camiccia garden, Bolinas, California

MORE ADVICE

Last but not least, I hope a few more tips will be helpful.

ANNUALS ARE EASY

Granted that advice is hardly needed for growing annuals since they only last a season and if they don't survive, you haven't lost much. But if your seashore garden is new and you want a supply of cut flowers for the house, annuals are your best bet. I think you should grow whichever flowers you like, but look for the ones that have been bred to have short stems—like the newer cosmos—since they are less likely to blow over than the original tall varieties. I've had modest good luck with annual salvia, short snapdragons, nasturtiums, and tall but thin and flexible *Verbena bonariensis*. I've never planted any annuals (or perennials either) where they would get the brunt of the wind.

But, as I said before, plant any annual you like, wherever you like, because the worst that will happen is that dies before it would die anyway.

Out of the wind, dahlias, cleome, cosmos, ageratum, nicotiana, and salvia thrive in a Massachusetts coastal cutting garden. Smith garden, Martha's Vineyard, Massachusetts. Design by John F. Hoff

GROUND COVERS

ajuga, *Ajuga genevensis*
barberry, *Berberis thunbergii*
beach wormwood, *Artemisia stelleriana*
bearberry, *Arctostaphylos uva-ursi*
bellflower, *Campanula takesimana* ‡
broom, *Genista pilosa*
candytuft, *Iberis sempervirens*
catmint, *Nepeta faassenii*
cotoneaster, *Cotoneaster*
crown vetch, *Coronilla varia* ‡ ‡
germander, *Teucrium chamaedrys*
goutweed, *Aegopodium podagraria* ‡ ‡
hay-scented fern, *Dennstaedtia punctilobula* ‡
heather, *Calluna*
junipers, many prostrate varieties
lamb's ears, *Stachys*
lavender cotton, *Santolina chamaecyparissus*
moss pink, *Phlox subulata*
rock rose, *Cistus salviifolius*
spurge, *Euphorbia myrsinites*
stonecrop, *Sedum acre*
sweet fern, *Comptonia peregrina*
thyme, *Thymus*
wintercreeper, *Euonymus fortunei* ‡

HERBS

basil	borage
chives	coriander
lavender	lemon verbena
marjoram	mint
nasturtium	oregano
parsley	rosemary
rue	sage
santolina	tarragon
thyme	winter savory

CHOOSE GROUND COVERS CAREFULLY

Before you decide to plant any of the ground covers, listed at left, check with your garden center or mail-order nursery to be sure it is hardy where you garden. If the botanical name has two words, only that species is the recommended plant. Ground covers that can become invasive are followed by the single symbol ‡. Two ‡‡ indicate "very invasive." Don't say you weren't warned.

HERBS THRIVE IN SEASHORE SUN

Since you've never seen an herb garden in the shade, in rich soil with lots of moisture, you can already guess that the sunny seashore with its thin, dry, and sandy or rocky soil is an ideal place to grow herbs. Try some of the ones listed at left, but first check to be sure which are annuals and which perennials are too tender for your garden. And remember that mint tends to run wild.

Iberis sempervirens

Santolina chamaecyparissus

A bountiful coastal Massachusetts herb and flower garden includes several kinds of
basil and rosemary, protected by a simple picket fence. Smetterer garden, Martha's Vineyard,
Massachusetts. Design by John F. Hoff

CAPTURE A VIEW

Not every seaside garden has a view, but for those of us lucky enough to have one, losing that view is the thing we worry most about. The worst part is that there is rarely anything we can do about it because what puts itself in your view usually doesn't belong to you. On top of that, many communities have become vigilant against homeowners and landscapers who clear-cut trees even on their own property, to get themselves a view. The view "solution" that I see most often is that of cutting the tops of the intruding trees, the way you would trim a hedge. That's futile, because those treetops will come back twice as thick as they were before. The best answer is to hire an experienced arborist and have him create view holes by taking out selective branches. Even a small "keyhole" can capture a worthwhile view.

This northern California garden shows how, with just enough protection, you can have both a view and a colorful border. Moss garden, Mendocino, California. Design by Gary Ratway

Brugmansia, 'Limelight' petunias, and Asiatic lilies with view beyond.
Campbell garden. Design by John F. Hoff

PLANTS FOR SEASHORE GARDENS

Ilex opaca f. *xanthocarpa*

Unless otherwise noted, the plants I include in this section are those that will survive in sun, wind, salt, and dry infertile soil. The symbol ∫ indicates a plant that can take these seashore elements without the protection of windbreaks or other barriers. Plants without the symbol are those that I and others grow in seashore places, sometimes without a clue about what makes them like this environment. If your neighbor is growing a plant you like, talk to your neighbor.

The zone listed at the end of each entry relates to the hardiness zone map at the back of the book. In some cases, as you will see, I list only one zone; that refers to the coldest areas where the plant will grow. Sometimes there are two, which refer to the coldest and warmest areas. Sometimes the difference is significant; other times it reflects only what I was able to find in reference books. In either case, it is important to note that hardiness zones may be less than accurate for seaside conditions. And as any experienced gardener knows, these are rules that can be broken, if you know what you are doing.

TREES AND SHRUBS

In this section I am primarily concerned with the trees and shrubs you can use to make windbreaks for the other plants in your garden. Trees and shrubs are where we seashore gardeners make our most expensive, discouraging mistakes; if we get these plants right, we'll be pretty sure to succeed with our gardens.

Most of the plants here are specific to certain areas, so be sure to check their regions against your own. What this means is that you need to consider each of the plants in this chapter individually and be careful about jumping to conclusions.

It seems too obvious to say this, but I will: plants native to your coastline will almost always outdo exotic imports. But now that I have

Acacia longifolia

said it, some of the very toughest seashore plants come from other places, even other continents. Acacias and *Acca*, the first trees in the plant directory, are a striking example of that.

Acacia cultriformis §
knife acacia

A bushy evergreen shrub, with yellow flowers in early spring, that can tolerate poor soil, heat, drought, and wind. Its deep roots will help anchor sandy banks and slopes. It grows to about 12 feet and makes a good windbreak. Zones 9 to 11.

Acacia longifolia §
Sydney golden wattle

This is a fast-growing large shrub or small tree from Australia, with spikes of yellow flowers in spring. It is highly resistant to strong winds and salt spray and an excellent plant for screening, especially along the California coast. It will grow in any soil, even almost pure sand. Its form is that of a loose mound, up to about 20 × 20 feet. Zone 8.

Acca sellowiana
pineapple guava

Native to Brazil and Uruguay, this South American fruit tree is planted in the United States for its showy summer flowers. It grows from 8 to 12 feet tall and equally wide, and can be used as a hedge. It tolerates dry sandy soil and salt spray, but not cold winds. Zones 8 to 10.

Acer pseudoplatanus §
sycamore maple

Sycamore maple tolerates wind and salt spray and grows well on both coasts. It is good for difficult spots, but it is not a tree for the South. William Flemer III, writing in his excellent book *Nature's Guide to Successful Gardening and Landscaping*, points out that after one hurricane, when all the other maples on Rhode Island shores lost their leaves, this tree appeared untouched. I am not aware of having ever seen one of these maples, but the New England Wild Flower Society lists this tree as invasive in Massachusetts, so you should check its status where you live before you plant. Zone 5.

Acca sellowiana

Acer pseudoplatanus

Alnus rubra
red alder

Alnus rubra is native from northern California to Alaska and grows best near the coast. If you have a salt marsh or another wet area on your property, this may be a good tree for you, since it tolerates salty brackish water and seasonal flooding. It does need water, so don't try it on a dry dune. Zones 7 to 10.

Alnus rubra

Amelanchier laevis

Amelanchier

serviceberry, shadbush

Most species of *Amelanchier* are native to North America. Since they hybridize freely, even some experts, I am told, have trouble telling them apart. They are graceful small trees or shrubs, with delicate white flowers that would be beautiful at any time. But for me, the greatest pleasure is to see them in early spring, lighting up the brown roadsides with their almost luminescent flowers that seem to come out of nowhere. The nickname "shadbush" comes from the fact that they bloom when the shad are running. *Amelanchier laevis*, in the photograph, is native to the Northeast, hardy from zones 4 to 8. *Amelanchier alnifolia*, a western native, is hardy from zones 2 to 7.

Arbutus menziesii

madrona

Madrona is a native broadleaf evergreen tree that grows along the Pacific coast from western British Columbia to Baja, California, sometimes right to the edge of the ocean. It requires sun and well-drained dryish soil and generally wants the Mediterranean climate of warm wet winters and dry summers. It is a valuable tree in the Pacific Northwest, and worth going to extreme lengths to save since it's notoriously difficult to plant and grow. Even the most minor changes in the soil, water, or compaction can kill the tree. Zone 8

Arctostaphylos patula §

green manzanita

This great evergreen California shrub may not be easy to find. It grows in sun or shade in poor soil, wind, and salt spray, up to 6 feet tall and just as wide. The 3-inch panicles of pink or white flowers bloom in late spring or summer. Zones 7 to 9.

Arctostaphylos uva-ursi §

bearberry, kinnikinick

Small shiny evergreen leaves and bright red berries on a stunning groundcover that is a little hard to get started. If you buy container-grown plants, put the root ball slightly above the soil, and mulch and water after planting, they will spread widely. Native to the Northeast and West Coast, *Arctostaphylos* doesn't do well in heat or humidity. Look for these cultivars: 'Massachusetts', 'Point Reyes', and 'Vancouver Jade'. Zone 3

Arbutus menziesii

Arctostaphylos patula

Arctostaphylos uva-ursi

Calluna vulgaris 'J. H. Hamilton'

Atriplex canescens

four-wing saltbush

Saltbush is a 3- to 5-foot evergreen shrub native to dry areas in the western United States. It has gray foliage and yellow flowers and can tolerate full sun, alkaline soil, sand, clay, and salt. It makes a ground cover or a specimen shrub and is a very good bird plant. Don't give this your best gardening conditions; it needs to be under some form of water stress, either from drought or salt. Zones 6 to 10.

Baccharis halimifolia §

groundsel tree, saltmarsh elder, sea myrtle

Not well known among gardeners, but an excellent 6-to-10-foot bush for a windbreak. Its white flowers bloom in summer and are followed on the female plants by clouds of silky white seed heads. Native from Massachusetts to Texas. Zone 6.

Calluna vulgaris

heather

These low evergreen shrubs are all one species, but with hundreds of cultivars. They need cool weather, excellent drainage, and sandy soil enriched with peat moss, but they can't take hot weather. They range from 6 to 24 inches in height and flower in late summer, in white, pink, lavender, or dusty purple. In winter, their green foliage may take on tones of gold, gray, reddish purple, and bronze. Zone 4.

Heathers are, however, unpredictable. Writing in his 1965 book, *Gardening by the Sea*, Daniel J. Foley introduces a detailed chapter on this plant by saying, "Of all the plants brought across the sea during the past 300 years, few have more romantic associations with the everyday life of bygone days than heather. Those who have walked the moors in the British Isles or on the Continent and picked their own nosegays of heather and gorse in the August sunshine have a very special kind of fondness for this plant of the wasteland. Curiously enough, this little shrub, steeped in sentiment and tradition, does not always take kindly to cultivation in our country. . . . They flourish in unexpected places in apparent neglect. . . . Yet many gardeners are bewildered when their beloved plants die, sometimes the first winter after planting." Ah, yes.

Ceanothus 'Concha'

Caryopteris ×*clandonensis* 'Longwood Blue'

Caryopteris ×*clandonensis*
bluebeard, blue mist

A small deciduous shrub, no more than 2 or 3 feet tall, with gray-green leaves and blue flowers that bloom in late summer and attract butterflies. Cut the branches to the ground each spring. Cultivars with showy flowers include 'Longwood Blue' and 'Blue Mist'. Zone 6.

Ceanothus

There are more than 50 species in this genus, most of them evergreen shrubs native to the West Coast. They bloom in early spring, when they are virtually smothered in blue flowers. They need dry, well-drained soil, which can be infertile since they fix their own nitrogen. They do need protection from the wind, and too much water will kill them. The average *Ceanothus* is about 6 feet tall, but they range from prostrate ground covers to 20-foot trees. *Ceanothus* 'Concha' is one of the best. Zones 7 or 8 to 10.

Ceanothus americanus

Chamaecyparis lawsoniana

Ceanothus americanus
New Jersey tea

One of the few *Ceanothus* species native to the East Coast, this summer-blooming, deciduous plant with white frothy flowers needs sun and sandy acidic soil with good drainage. It is native to the New Jersey Pine Barrens, among other places from Quebec to Texas and Florida. Prune it hard in early spring to keep it looking its best. Zones 4 to 9.

Chamaecyparis lawsoniana §
Lawson cypress, Port Orford cedar

This very large tall old tree is native to a relatively small area along the West Coast from southern Oregon to northern California. Of all the major forest trees in North America, this one has suffered most from human activity. Nearly all the old-growth forests have been logged and an introduced root rot is taking the rest. Although the news for the natural tree is bad, this is an excellent tree for gardens because of its many cultivars. These come in many shapes and sizes; the dwarf ones make good

Comptonia peregrina

Clethra alnifolia 'Hummingbird'

hedges. Lawson cypress needs sun but is tolerant of poor soil and coastal weather. Zone 7.

Clethra alnifolia
sweet pepperbush, summer sweet

The natural species grows to about 8 feet tall, although some cultivars are shorter. In the wild, *Clethra* grows in swampy or poorly drained soil; in the garden, it needs regular watering. It can take salt spray. Mine dropped its needy roots next to the outdoor shower, which brought the heavenly scent of its flowers to my bedroom window. It couldn't have worked out better if I had planted it myself. Zones 4 to 9.

Comptonia peregrina
sweet fern

One summer, about a dozen years ago, I first noticed a patch of short ferny plants that weren't ferns, no more than 3 feet tall, next to my driveway. I don't know when they first arrived—presumably they didn't all show up at once—but I was delighted to be introduced to the aromatic bush called sweet fern. It is reported to have played a part in various Native American ceremonies, and Daniel Foley wrote in 1965 that "earlier generations of boys used to collect the leaves and dry them as substitutes for tobacco." It is said to grow well in gravelly and sandy soil, and its roots are good binders in sand. Nevertheless a few years later, when I looked for it, my sweet fern had disappeared. I don't know where it came from or why it left, but I'd be happy to have it again. The only place I've seen it for sale is at www.Horticopia.com.

Cryptomeria japonica 'Cristata'   *Cupressus macrocarpa*

Cryptomeria japonica §

This beautiful conifer doesn't seem to be on anyone's list of seashore plants, but in driving around Martha's Vineyard one April, and noticing how many of the cedars and junipers were marred by the unusually bitter cold and wind of the past winter, I was amazed to see these much more beautiful trees looking so fresh and pristine. They are reputed to do well on seacoasts, like the humidity, and can't take drought or sparse rainfall. If you have moist acid soil, there is to my mind no more beautiful conifer for a garden. 'Lobbii' is a compact cultivar. Zones 6 to 8.

Cupressus macrocarpa §
Monterey cypress

This is the picturesque Monterey cypress with the distinctive wind-swept profile that I used to assume was a typical tree of the Pacific coast. In fact, there are only two natural stands of *Cupressus macrocarpa*, one on the north side of Carmel Bay, California, and a smaller one on the south side of the bay. However, the tree has been widely planted throughout the California coastal area as a hedge or windbreak. Unless it is scrupulously pruned twice a year, the youngster shoots up into a rough, unmanageable tree. Sally Robinson gives firsthand advice on her problems with this tree in the chapter "Gardens at the Shore." Zones 8 and 9.

Elaeagnus commutata
silverberry

Elaeagnus is a name that raises warning signals ("Invasive!") to conscientious gardeners, but this one is recommended by William Cullina, of the New England Wild Flower Society, author of several books on native plants. In *Native Trees, Shrubs, & Vines,* he compares it to its weedy cousins from the Old World that have run amok and become scourges in the East. In contrast to their dirty gray leaves, silverberry's leaves are strikingly beautiful, "dressed in silky pewter, that shines softly in the sun." Cullina considers it one of our most beautiful foliage shrubs. It's not as aggressive as the Russian and autumn olives, but it does have running roots, which makes it ideal for stabilizing banks and sandy or gravelly soil. It grows between 1 and 7 feet tall. Zones 2 to 6, in sun.

Elaeagnus commutata

Gaultheria shallon §
salal

Salal is an evergreen shrub native to the Pacific Northwest. In the wild, it grows into impenetrable thickets of glossy leaves that are often used in flower arrangements. It makes a rugged windscreen up to 10 feet high. Its aggressive underground runners are good holders in sand, but don't plant this one near your house. Zones 6 to 8.

Gaultheria shallon

Genista lydia

Gleditsia triacanthos

Hebe speciosa 'Violacea'

Genista lydia

broom, woadwaxen

This member of the pea family is closely related to *Cytisus*, with similar yellow flowers, gray-green stems, and blue-green leaves. Also called woadwaxen, this species is only about 2 feet tall. It grows in poor sandy or gravelly soil and can stand drought but not humidity. The great advantage of the *Genista* over the *Cytissus* brooms is that these are not invasive and the others are. Zones 6 to 8.

Gleditsia triacanthos §

honey locust

Although it is native to rich bottomlands along the East Coast, honey locusts will thrive in wind, salt spray, drought, and sandy soil. The lacy leaves turn a glowing gold in the fall. Wild trees have amazing thorns and huge curved seed pods that make them a big cleanup problem in a conventional garden but possibly a benefit if the tree is part of your hedge or wind barrier. Zone 4.

Hebe

Hebe is a large genus of mostly evergreen low-growing shrubs and ground covers, named for the Greek goddess of youth. Native to the coastal areas of New Zealand, they tolerate poor soil, pollution, salt, and coastal winds. Where it is very hot, grow them in part shade; otherwise they'll do well in sun. Zones 9 and 10.

Heteromeles salicifolia

Christmas berry, toyon

An evergreen shrub or small tree native to California and the southwest corner of Oregon, toyon is drought tolerant but fire resistant if watered every two weeks during the spring and summer. At about 7 feet tall and 5 feet wide, it makes an excellent screen or hedge plant. It grows naturally in beach sand. White flowers bloom in summer and the red berries from which it gets its name appear from November through January. Zone 8 to 10.

Heteromeles salicifolia var. *cerina*

Hudsonia tomentosa

Hippophae rhamnoides §
sea buckthorn

This is a rugged shrub, with a handsome display of showy yellow flowers, that can take all the coastal conditions you have to offer: dry sandy soil, wind, and salt spray. You can prune it if you want to use it as an unusual specimen, but it has yet another virtue, dense growth and thorns that makes it a safety barrier hedge if you need one. It's not easy to find, but at least one Canadian nursery sells this plant on the Internet. (You can also find lots of places that make it into skin creams.) Zone 4.

Hudsonia tomentosa §
beach heather

This native dune plant of the Northeast states is not something you can buy or transplant, so this information is for anyone lucky enough to have this low gray sand plant on the property. As propagator for the New England Wild Flower Society, William Cullina has had "less than satisfactory success" with *Hudsonia* once it is taken out of its sand-scoured environment. The "nested buns" grow in pure sand, sending their roots down until they receive a steady supply of moisture. *Hudsonia* grows about 2 inches a year and stays just above the sand that continues to blow over them. For two weeks in June, my dry dunes are covered with starry yellow flowers. Zones 2 to 8.

Hydrangea macrophylla

Hydrangea macrophylla

I find few things more evocative of a New England coastal resort town in August than the sight of masses of these luscious "mophead" shrubs in shades of blue running even up into purple. Old-fashioned hydrangeas go in and out of favor, but I doubt if any of us will outlive our current love affair with these beautiful plants. And to think they will grow by the sea!

There are two forms of *macrophylla*, both about 6 feet tall and 8 feet wide. The hortensias have heavy round mopheads of sterile flowers; the lace-caps have flat heads composed of tiny fertile flowers surrounded by the showier sterile flowers.

As you probably know, the color of *Hydrangea* depends on the pH of the soil—generally blue in soil of about 5.5; purple in more acid soil; and pink in alkaline soil. *Hydrangea* thrives in wind and salt, but can't take drought. In late winter, prune off last season's flower heads to the stem's uppermost bud. Zones 6 to 9.

Ilex

Although those lucky Pacific Northwest gardeners are the only ones who can grow the most beautiful English holly, there are good hollies for the rest of us in this marvelous group of shrubs that can take the wind and salt of the coast.

Ilex aquifolium
English holly

This is a beautiful, salt-tolerant evergreen tree, but better in the cool humid weather of the Pacific coast, like its native England, than elsewhere. Zones 7 to 9.

Ilex opaca
American holly

Not quite as beautiful or salt tolerant as English holly but more heat and cold hardy, evergreen American holly grows wild from Massachusetts to Florida and is well suited to the West Coast too. It tolerates drought, sandy soil, and salt air. The leaves are lighter in color than those of its English relative, with a matte finish. Male trees can have darker shiny leaves, but both male and female trees are necessary to get the orange-red berries. Several cultivars have prettier leaves and berries than the wild plants have. Yellow-fruited forms are often called *xanthocarpa*. 'Canary' has spiny leaves and orange-yellow berries. Zone 6 to 9.

Ilex vomitoria §
yaupon holly

Yaupon is a fast-growing evergreen shrub or small tree, native of the southeastern United States, very tolerant of drought and salt. It is often trimmed into hedges, and useful for protective screening. With its evergreen foliage and very large crops of persistent red berries, it is a handsome landscape plant and an important food for wildlife. Zones 8 to 10.

Juniperus virginiana §
eastern red cedar

Most junipers are easy, trouble-free trees and shrubs for seaside conditions. Eastern red cedar is a tough evergreen tree found throughout the eastern United States. It makes a fast screen and its berries are attractive to birds. The species grows to 30 feet, but cultivars, with more attractive foliage, range in height from 3 feet up. *Juniperus horizontalis*, creeping juniper, has such salt-tolerant cultivars as 'Bar Harbor' and 'Blue Rug'. Zone 2.

Several junipers make excellent ground covers for the shore: *J. con-*

Ilex opaca 'Canary'

Juniperus conferta

Ilex vomitoria

Juniperus virginiana 'Burkii'

ferta, shore juniper, no more than 1 to 2 feet tall, can even be used to stabilize sand dunes. Zone 6.

Myrica

Three shrubs in this genus are among the must useful plants for the windy shorelines of the United States. They are all well adapted to dry, infertile sandy soil and salt spray.

Myrica californica
California bayberry, Pacific wax myrtle

An evergreen shrub or a small tree that can reach 20 feet. The leaves are dark green and aromatic when crushed. The purplish berries covered with white wax cover the stems in fall and are prized by birds. Native along the Pacific coast from Canada south. Zones 7 to 9.

Myrica cerifera
southern bayberry, wax myrtle.

A similar shrub to northern bayberry, with lighter green leaves and gray berries. This evergreen species is native along the Atlantic coast from Maryland south. It ranges in height from about 8 to 20 feet. Zones 7 to 9.

Myrica californica

Nerium oleander, 'Petite Pink'

Myrica pensylvanica

Myrica pensylvanica
bayberry

In the Northeast, this native deciduous shrub, rarely more than 6 feet tall, is emblematic of the coast. Its gray berries (on the female plants) are the basis for New England's famous bayberry candles. The berries persist on the plants after the leaves turn purple and drop in fall. An excellent addition to a protective border on inland dunes. In *Native Trees, Shrubs, & Vines*, William Cullina says he always recommends this instead of the grow-anywhere invasives like Japanese barberry and winged euonymus. Zones 4 to 7.

Nerium oleander §
oleander

A handsome evergreen poisonous shrub that grows up to 12 feet tall and blooms all summer in drought. salt, heat, and wind, which makes it ideal for a Southeast seashore garden. It is used extensively for screening along beaches. The species has red berries, but cultivars come in different heights and colors. The lovely 'Petite Pink' grows to only 3 or 4 feet. *All parts of the plant are poisonous; even smoke from the wood can irritate.* Zones 8 to 9.

Nyssa sylvatica

Nyssa sylvatica
tupelo, black gum, sour gum, beetlebung

Native from Maine to Florida. This is one of my favorite trees, with beautiful horizontal spiky branches and leaves that turn an absolutely stunning range of colors in early fall, from apricot through every shade of red and purple. It is said to require wet soil, and grows even out to the water's edge in sandy soil, but it is just as beautiful on our dry inland dunes. On Martha's Vineyard—and nowhere else as far as I know—it is called the beetlebung tree. Apparently the tough wood was once used to make corks for the bungholes in wine barrels. According to my dictionary, a beetle is a wooden hammer. Since this tree doesn't transplant well, buy container plants. Beetlebung looks best in a clump. Zone 3.

Phoenix canariensis
Canary Island date palm

A slow-growing palm with a thick trunk and a handsome umbrella of arching fronds; very tolerant of dry soil, heat, and drought. Severe frost can kill the leaves. Zone 9.

Picea glauca 'Arneson's Blue'

Phoenix canariensis

Picea glauca

white spruce

This salt-resistant North American native is useful as a windbreak or a screen. It is an excellent tree for the cold, but not for heat. More commonly grown are the dwarf species like 'Arneson's Blue'. Zone 3.

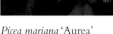
Picea mariana 'Aurea'

Pinus contorta

Picea mariana §
black spruce

This is one of the hardiest of all spruces, native all across Canada, from Newfoundland to Alaska. It thrives in the coldest climates and is singularly tolerant of salt spray and fierce storms. Although it can take heat and dryness, it needs winter cold. It is the typical tree of the Maine coast and the Maritime provinces. Zone 2.

Pinus contorta §
lodgepole pine, shore pine

This species has two forms, the tall lodgepole pine and the shorter bushy shore pine, which is sometimes called *Pinus contorta* var. *contorta*. Although short-lived, shore pine is extremely tolerant of salt, sand, and strong winds. It is widespread on both the inner and outer shores of the Northwest coast. It grows from the coast of Alaska to northern California on dunes, seaside bluffs, and exposed rocky headlands. Depending on the site, it reaches heights of 20 to 50 feet. It is an ideal tree for a multi-species windbreak on the Pacific coast. Zone 7

Pittosporum tobira

Pinus thunbergii

Pinus halepensis §
Aleppo pine

A fast-growing multi-trunked tree that can reach 50 or 60 feet. It has gray-green needles and a windswept look even when young. It is very tolerant of seashore conditions—wind, salt spray, heat, and drought. Zone 8.

Pinus thunbergii §
Japanese black pine

This has long been the first choice for seaside conditions on both coasts, but Cornell University is no longer recommending it for the East Coast because it is being decimated by a borer. In all honesty, losing these trees no longer bothers me as much as it once did, since young healthy ones spring up so quickly. While I wouldn't buy new trees, I still think they are perfect for a seashore garden. If you are interested in planting them, you probably should check with a nursery or with the extension service in your area first. Zone 6.

Pittosporum tobira §
Japanese mock orange

A handsome seaside shrub with leathery leaves and fragrant spring flowers. It grows from 6 to 15 feet tall and makes an excellent hedge in sun or shade. It withstands wind, salt, and drought. This species can be sheared to control its size or shape. 'Variegata' has white-edged leaves and grows no higher than 5 feet. 'Wheeler's Dwarf' is 2 feet tall. Zones 9 and 10.

Prunus maritima

Prunus maritima
beach plum

Along with bayberry, beach plum is the ubiquitous shrub of the dry dunes of coastal New England. Its native range is from New Brunswick to Maryland. When it is in bloom in spring, the roadsides are white with its showy flowers. On Martha's Vineyard in the late summer those same roadsides are populated by jelly makers collecting the small purple or, more rarely, yellow fruits for our famous beach plum jelly. In the wild, beach plum is a pretty scraggly shrub, but if you want to use it in a garden, and give it water and pruning when it needs it, beach plum can be a perfectly respectable shrub. Don't try to dig one from the wild; as one writer said, the roots of all beach plums go back to a single plant on Cape Cod. Zones 3 to 6.

Pyracantha coccinea 'Mohave'

Pyracantha

This very decorative, popular garden plant is not one for the front line, but if you water it well at first, it can survive drought. The cultivar 'Mohave' is a heavy-berried disease-resistant variety. Zone 7.

Quercus virginiana

Rhus typhina

Quercus virginiana
live oak

One of the South's great trees, this broad, tall, evergreen oak is native to the shores of the southeast coast from Virginia to Florida. It grows quickly when young, slowing down to become a massive tree, often wider than it is tall. Live oaks are susceptible to freeze damage, but are highly tolerant of salt spray, and even tolerant of hurricane force winds and heavy rains. Despite their reputation, many live oaks, some as much as 300 years old, were downed in the devastating four hurricanes that hit Florida in 2004. Zones 7 or 8 to 10.

Rhus typhina
staghorn sumac

Although the genus *Rhus* contains such unpleasant species as poison ivy, poison oak, and poison sumac, all the plants listed here are completely harmless. They can take wind and salt spray and drought when they are established. *Rhus typhina* is similar to a number of other sumac species, including *glabra* and *copallina*, native to the eastern United States. All these shrubs form thickets of erect stems. They color up beautifully in autumn, when they display their large red staghorns. Zone 4.

Rosa

If the only rose that graced the seashore were *Rosa rugosa*, it would be *dayenu* ("enough"), as the Jewish Passover song says. And while *Rosa rugosa* is uniquely adapted to the harshest environment, fully equipped to be the first line of defense along an open beach, and the parent of many cultivars, a surprising number of other roses will thrive with some protection. Rose expert Peter Schneider writes that the best roses for the shore are those that are bushy as opposed to the hybrid teas that grow bolt upright. Writing in the *Taylor's Guide to Seashore Gardening*, he says, "When a naturally bushy variety makes shorter growth, it still looks like a bush. When an upright variety makes shorter growth, it looks like a stick." The roses listed here are only those I have personally grown, or tried to grow.

Rosa 'Betty Prior'

Rosa 'American Pillar'

This is an old rambler that I inherited from a friend—my mother took a small rooted piece and willed it to grow at my new, plantless house. It has for years, although I never knew what it was until I read an editorial about it in the *Vineyard Gazette* by the paper's distinguished editor, Henry Beetle Hough. It has large clusters of single dark pink flowers with white eyes. It is hardy and disease free; blooms in late summer. Schneider says it is a great favorite.

Rosa 'Betty Prior'

In late summer, when I go downtown, or, as we say, down island, I marvel at the bright blooming 'Betty Prior' roses that seem to be everywhere. Schneider particularly recommends these for the Pacific coast, where roses with lots of petals refuse to open in the fog. He says, 'Betty Prior', a floribunda, has "pretty dogwoodlike blooms that give no hint of the variety's toughness." I like to think that the reason my rose died was that I planted it just before a bitter cold winter that killed so many of our "hardy" plants. Zone 4.

Rosa rugosa

Rosa rugosa
beach rose

It's not likely that you would want to grow only one plant in your seaside garden, but if you did, this would be the one. An accidental stowaway off a Japanese ship in the late nineteenth century, this rose has so naturalized itself along the New England coastline that most people assume it is a native plant. It is extraordinarily hardy, grows in pure sand, and tolerates wind and salt spray. You can cut it to the ground every year as designer Nan Sinton, whose work is presented in the chapter "Gardens at the Shore," did with her long border; or you can let it grow to its natural height of 4 to 6 feet. The magenta flowers bloom in June with occasional repeats all summer. The large orange hips are high in vitamin C and some people, like my daughter, think they are edible. Others make them into a sweet bland jam. The epithet *rugosa* refers to its rugose, or wrinkled, leaves. The rose is resistant to disease and even if it does come down with something, it will outgrow it on its own. Never use chemical sprays; they do more harm than good. The cultivar 'Alba' is beautiful, and there are many other cultivars. Zone 4.

Sabal palmetto

Rosmarinus officinalis 'Arp'

Rosmarinus officinalis
rosemary

This is one of those delightful herbs that everyone I know wishes they could grow. It needs sun, thrives in poor soil, and tolerates heat, wind, salt spray, and drought. At the most it will reach 4 feet tall, and the more you prune it for culinary use, the better it grows. It's a particularly good plant for the Pacific Northwest. Zones 8 to 10; zone 7 with protection.

Sabal palmetto §
cabbage palm

A Southeast native palm, *Sabal palmetto*, the state tree of South Carolina and Florida, grows to about 50 feet. It grows from the North Carolina barrier islands down to the Florida keys and up the Gulf coast to the Florida panhandle. It is very salt- and drought-tolerant and can be used in beachside plantings. The name comes from the fact that the early settlers boiled the tender heart and claimed it tasted like cabbage—or like sauerkraut if it was fermented. Zones 7 to 10.

Syringa vulgaris

Tamarix ramosissima

Trachycarpus fortunei

Syringa vulgaris
lilac

There is probably no one who doesn't know the common lilac, with its beautiful and fragrant spring flowers. This is, however, a good time to bring up the issue of mildew, since if anything in your garden is going to get mildew, lilac will be it (followed, no doubt, by phlox). I think it just depends on your climate. For me, one of the joys of seashore gardening is that my plants *don't* get mildewed. Unlike the lilacs in Cambridge, where I live most of the year, and whose blooms are followed by ugly mildewed leaves, none of my plants on Martha's Vineyard suffers from mildew. I've always assumed that it is the salt in the air that accounts for it, but that can't be the only thing, since seashore areas that also have heat, humidity, and fog are also home to mildewed plants. This is another case where looking at the plants in your neighbors' gardens can help you make the right decisions. Most lilacs need cold winters to bloom. Zone 4.

Tamarix ramosissima §
salt cedar, tamarisk

A tough shrub, tolerant of sand and salt, that grows from 6 to 10 feet in height and is useful for a windbreak. It has fine-textured foliage and fluffy pink flowers in summer. In spite of the delicacy of its leaves and flowers, tamarisk is a tough plant with deep roots and shouldn't be planted near sewers or water pipes. You can prune it in early spring since the flowers appear on new wood and you can renew an old bush by cutting it to the ground. Zone 6.

Trachycarpus fortunei
windmill palm

An import from China, this is the most cold hardy palm in North America. It survives in temperatures as low as 5 degrees, and is widely used on Vancouver Island. It's no more than 20 feet tall, and easy to grow. Zone 8.

Umbellularia californica with lavender

Vaccinium corymbosum in fruit and fiery
fall leaf color.

Umbellularia californica
California laurel, Oregon myrtle

Umbellularia is a slow-growing evergreen tree that can be pruned as a shrub. It is related to the Greek laurel we use in cooking, and can be substituted for that. Its native range runs from California into Oregon. The tree litters a lot and has invasive roots, two attributes that are negative in a formal garden but a great benefit when the plant is used in a protective planting along the shore. Zones 7 to 10.

Vaccinium corymbosum
highbush blueberry

Everything about this bush, native to the Northeast, is beautiful: the pinkish flowers in spring, the delicious berries, which you'll have to share with the birds, in summer, and the brilliant foliage in fall. It needs fertile acidic soil with plenty of mulch to protect its shallow roots. Lowbush blueberry, *Vaccinium angustifolium*, another native, is a great ground cover for similar conditions. Both are hardy to zone 3.

A Northwest native is the evergreen huckleberry, *Vaccinium ovatum*, which grows to 6 feet in coastal forests. Zone 7.

Viburnum

There are so many species and cultivars of *Viburnum*, and they are such marvelous shrubs, that the best advice I can give is to check your local supplier, look at the plant in flower, or read all the specs in a catalog, and then choose the ones that appeal to you. Natives to your area will obviously do well, but there are many cultivars that may suit your conditions. To be safe, give them some protection from the wind and supply a thick mulch to keep the roots cool. Flowering viburnum, *V. nudum* 'Winterthur', is a Pennsylvania Horticultural Society award winner. Zones 5 to 9.

Above: *Viburnum nudum* 'Winterthur'. Right: *Viburnum wrightii*

Gelsemium sempervirens

Parthenocissus quinquefolia in fall color, with *Spiraea japonica* and *Sedum* 'Autumn Joy'

VINES

Whether you need a protective "fence" or a ground cover, vines can be both useful and attractive in a seashore garden. But if you live in California or the Pacific Northwest, be careful to avoid the ivies; some of them, originally brought in to protect the dunes, have turned out to be invasive.

Gelsemium sempervirens
Carolina jasmine

A decorative evergreen vine with fragrant yellow flowers, native from Virginia to Texas. But don't eat it—all parts are poisonous. Carolina jasmine can climb to 20 feet, twining around any supports it can get its tendrils on, but to keep it under control and bushier, prune it after it flowers. It tolerates hot sun, wind, and salt spray. Zone 8.

Parthenocissus quinquefolia

Virginia creeper, woodbine

If you have any junk cars or old appliances on your property, you can easily hide them with Virginia creeper, a native vine that will grow virtually anywhere and climb over anything. Its greatest claim to our attention is that it is the first plant to change color in the fall, and the color it turns is beautiful flaming red. It grows up trees and over bushes on my dry dunes, and I've seen it even at the ocean shore. The only place I wouldn't want it is on a very small plot of land; it can grow 4 to 8 feet in a single season. Of course, if you have chain-link fence, it's a perfect cover. Don't let it grow against wood. Ironically, this beautiful wild vine is often confused with poison ivy. But if you remember that poison ivy has three leaves and "quinquefolia" means five-leaved, you should never confuse the two again. Zones 4 to 9.

Achillea 'Coronation Gold'

PERENNIALS

The perennials in this section have several things in common that make them suitable for a windy site. They don't have large single petals that would get tattered in the wind. Nor do they sit on tall slender stems that would snap in that wind. They need sun to be at their best and they usually do well in dry infertile soil, not the rich moist soil that most garden perennials like. These are only a smattering of the plants that will thrive on a coastal site, but they epitomize the features that you should look for in other perennials if your garden is unprotected—or almost unprotected—from wind and salt. But now that I've said that, you'll notice that I've included a few of my favorite plants that don't meet those "essential" requirements. I don't have them in the brunt of the wind, but definitely at the seashore.

Achillea

yarrow

These hardy perennials tolerate poor soil and dryness very well; their tiny flowers are crowded in flat clusters, and the new hybrids offer plants in many lovely shades of pink, orange, salmon, and red as well as yellow. 'Coronation Gold' and 'Paprika' are two of many hybrids. Yarrows bloom in summer. Zone 3.

Achillea millefolium 'Paprika'

Armeria maritima 'Splendens'

Artemisia 'Powis Castle'

Asclepias tuberosa 'Gay Butterflies'

Armeria maritima

sea pink, common thrift

Neat little globes of pinkish flowers atop erect 6-to-8-inch stems make an easy, cheerful early summer addition to the perennial border. It looks right in a coast garden, which may be why it carries its name. Zones 3 to 8.

Artemisia 'Powis Castle'

Most of the hundreds of species of *Artemisia* have silvery or gray aromatic foliage and grow well in sandy, infertile soil; they tolerate drought and salt spray, but not wet soil or humidity. 'Powis Castle' makes a large mound of finely textured silver foliage about 3 feet tall and 4 feet wide. Zones 5 to 8.

Artemisia schmidtiana

silver mound

This silvery mound, no more than 4 to 12 inches high, looks far too delicate to be out in the weather, yet in my garden it was hardier than the 'Powis Castle' that I tried to accommodate for a few years before I gave its place to Ms. "Schmidtiana." Zones 3 to 7.

Asclepias tuberosa

butterfly weed

A stunning member of the milkweed family, native throughout the eastern United States, butterfly weed likes sandy soil and grows only about 2 feet tall. It blooms in summer. Although it's a tough little plant, its roots are crooked and brittle, which makes transplanting it difficult. Better to buy a new seedling and leave the plant you have alone. Zone 3.

Baptisia australis

false indigo

A beautiful American wildflower that makes a large round clump 3 to 4 feet tall and 4 to 6 feet wide. The foliage is blue green, and the deep blue late spring flowers are followed by interesting large black seedpods. This is a long-lasting easy plant and although I've never grown it in the face of a full wind, with a little protection it does very well, with the shape of a neat, well -rounded shrub. Actually, this is a plant that grows better in wind and sand than in quiet air and rich soil, which would make it too tall and floppy. Zone 3.

Baptisia australis

Echinacea purpurea

Hemerocallis 'Stella de Oro'

Euphorbia characias subsp. *wulfenii*

Echinacea purpurea
purple coneflower

A handsome native wildflower that blooms from early to midsummer. The protruding purple cone is surrounded by drooping pinkish daisylike petals. The sturdy plant grows 2 to 4 feet tall in sun in average soil. A number of cultivars, with flatter faces or a more compact stance, as well as in white, are available. For me this is one of those if-it-ain't-broke-don't-fix-it plants. I'm delighted to have the original. Zones 3 to 9.

Euphorbia characias
spurge

Spurge dropped in on me, stayed a few years, and then disappeared. I hope it visited someone else, since I found it unusual and delightful. The only facts I know about it come from a British Web page that calls it "hardy." Mediterranean spurge (subspecies *wulfenii*) grows up to 4 feet tall. Mine must have been a wild one; it never grew more than 12 inches. Tall enough for me.

Hemerocallis
daylily

I have no idea what makes this such a good perennial for the shore, but I've never had one that didn't thrive with a modicum of protection. There are so many hybrids that you could choose a different one each year and never run out of new plants. But if you want to start with one, I recommend 'Stella de Oro'. It is short, only a foot tall, and reblooms; you'll have flowers on and off all summer. Zone 4

Nepeta ×*faassenii*
catmint

One of the most attractive and useful plants for a seashore garden, especially when used to show off other flowers. It makes a handsome low clump 1 to 2 feet tall and just as wide, with blue flowers that last for weeks in early summer. If you cut it back, you should get a second display, not quite as good as the first one. *Nepeta* 'Six Hills Giant' is a larger cultivar. Zones 4 to 8.

Nepeta ×*faassenii*

Opuntia littoralis var. *austrocalifornica*

Opuntia littoralis
prickly pear cactus

I have trouble thinking of cactus growing anywhere other than in our Southwest desert, but obviously I am wrong. *Opuntia littoralis*, coastal prickly pear cactus, zone 9, is native to southern California and Mexico. *Opuntia humifusa*, zone 4, is native from Massachusetts to Georgia. Both seem to like the seashore where they tolerate dry sandy soil and salt spray.

Perovskia atriplicifolia
Russian sage

A newly popular plant that is particularly good in a coastal garden since it needs full sun and very well drained, preferably poor, sandy soil. It may take a few years to get established but when it does you'll have a 3-to-5-foot cloud of aromatic silvery foliage and panicles of tiny blue to lavender flowers. Zones 5 to 9; zone 4 with protection.

Perovskia atriplicifolia

Platycodon grandiflorus 'Sentimental Blue'

Platycodon grandiflorus
balloon flower, platycodon

Year after year, this is the bluest, showiest, most dependable, least fussy perennial in my garden, where it is growing at the edge of an increasingly dappled shade bed. It grows 2 feet tall in clumps, and if you deadhead, you'll have flowers from early summer till the end of August. In addition to the pure blue flowers, you can get *Platycodon* in pale pink or white, but why would you want to? In rich soil and too much shade, *Platycodon* need staking. Mine has no bad habits. Zones 3 to 8.

Sedum 'Autumn Joy'

Sedum 'Autumn Joy'
autumn joy

A very popular *Sedum* hybrid that never spreads or becomes invasive as some others do. 'Autumn Joy' grows in 2-foot-tall, 2-foot-wide clumps, with round heads of densely packed flowers. Think of broccoli. The flower heads start out as light green in summer, turn dark pink, and then age to brown and stay on the plant all winter. Zones 3 to 9.

GRASSES

Cady Goldfield, whose wisdom is also featured in "Advice from Seashore Gardeners," is a landscape designer who lives and practices on the north shore of Massachusetts, and specializes in grasses and bamboos in her work. She points out that grasses are pioneer plants, the first to colonize new open spaces after the lichens and mosses, and so are designed to deal with exposure. "Aesthetically," she says, "grasses play along with coastal conditions. They have movement that mirrors the movement of the ocean itself. Watching a stand of mounded 'moppy' grasses as it shimmers and undulates in the wind is sensually appealing. And the accompanying rustling and whispering of sound, especially from grasses with big seed heads, such as northern sea oats, is dramatic."

Grasses come in a great many varieties and forms; before planting any, you might want to check to be sure the grass you choose meets these qualifications: it should be a perennial, not an annual; hardy in your zone; and, if you live in the South, one that can stand the heat. You want a grass that isn't fazed by wind and salt and won't get smashed down by rain or other bad weather. If you want to use grasses as a protective hedge, selections with running roots are fine; otherwise be sure you get clumping grasses. You probably don't want grasses that become invasive by seeding themselves because you can't control where the seeds will light.

Grasses, for our purpose, come in three different varieties: bamboos, dune grasses, and ornamental grasses.

BAMBOO

If you're interested in less recognized plants for your seashore garden, you might want to try bamboo. When I started writing this book, bamboo wasn't on any plant list I saw. Since then, I've found a few gardeners who use it. Along with other grasses, Cady Goldfield has been experimenting with bamboos, and offers her advice about using them to shelter other plants in a windy area, but only after the bamboo itself is established. She recommends protecting young bamboo by staking around it and then running burlap or other screening around the stakes to make a protective "corral" around the grove. After a couple of winters, the grove should be strong enough to withstand winter coastal winds on its own without protection; however, leaves on outer culms will probably get burnt by wind or sun in very cold, windy, and sunny winters. That is typical and shouldn't cause concern. Fresh foliage will grow in the spring. Goldfield, who gardens in the northeast, has had no problems

Bambusa vulgaris

Semiarundinaria fastuosa

with invasiveness. In zones 5 and 6 even the most aggressive bamboos do not gain as much ground as they do in milder climates. The soil warms more slowly here (except in microclimates) and limits the shooting time for the bamboos. Usually it's not difficult to keep the bamboos under control by mowing, cutting, or kicking down unwanted shoots that come up in inconvenient places.

Pseudosasa japonica
arrow bamboo

This is the best bamboo to start with because it is well suited to the windy shore. An import from the coastal areas of Japan, arrow bamboo can take fog, wind, and salt spray; it grows to a height of 18 feet and has wide leaves that make a good screen or hedge. You should have no trouble locating it; it's one of the most widespread bamboos for sale in this country. Zone 7.

Bambusa vulgaris
common bamboo

An ornamental timber bamboo whose culm, although starchy and relatively soft, is used in construction and as a choice source for paper. *Bambusa vulgaris* will spread relatively fast and easily, is edible, and is the one you'll most often find for your garden.

Semiarundinaria fastuosa
temple bamboo

A mid-size temperate bamboo for full sun, *Semiarundaria fastuosa* is the tallest and stateliest of its genus and the largest hardy bamboo for the Pacific Northwest coast. Although supposedly reaching 35 feet, its top height here is 25 feet. Its erect narrow form makes it a good choice for a screen or a hedge, or any area where arching fronds would be intrusive. The variety *viridis* has vivid, dark green culms and branches, which retain their color in the sun, and even into old age. Zones 6 to 10.

DUNE GRASSES

With the exception of American beach grass, most native dune grasses aren't easy to purchase in the quantities of small sizes that you would need to plant a dune. But if you have a dune and want a natural planting, they can be found with some effort and ingenuity.

Ammophila breviligulata
American beach grass

American beach grass is a native of the mid-Atlantic coast from Maine to North Carolina, and around the shores of the Great Lakes. It is a cool season perennial grass that grows in pure sand and wind-driven salt; it can spread 6 to 10 feet each year, catching as much as a foot of sand over its stems. This ability makes dunes grow and protects the stability of shore communities. American beach grass is the plant used in Atlantic dune restorations, and you can often get plants from the beach conservation organizations in your area. Zone 3

On the West Coast, the story is different. There, as has so often happened, good intentions have led to a disastrous outcome; an excellent plant in one area has become an invasive one in another. American beach grass and European beach grass, *Ammophila arenaria*, were imported to stabilize dunes on the West Coast. There both grasses spread so aggressively as to change the dune shapes, plant communities, and animal habitats along Washington's southwest coast. They have virtually overcome

Ammophila breviligulata

Leymus mollis, the dominant grass along the Washington dunes before the arrival of the two *Ammophila*.

Panicum amarum

panic grass, bitter switchgrass

A clump-forming, dune-stabilizing beach grass native to sandy coastal areas from Connecticut to Florida and Texas. It grows in dry sand between the front and back dunes. 'Dewey Blue' is a handsome cultivar that grows 3 to 4 feet tall. It is noted for its powder blue foliage and fountainlike form. It may flop over in rich soil. Zones 2 to 9.

Uniola paniculata

sea oats

Sea oats, a Florida native, once covered the dunes and beaches from North Carolina to south Florida; today they are an endangered species and it is illegal in their home state even to pick them. They are attractive grasses to plant on the dunes and extremely useful for dune preservation. Even a small plant may have roots reaching 5 feet beneath the sand. Zone 7.

Miscanthus sinensis 'Cabaret'

Festuca glauca

Ornamental grasses

Relatively speaking, grasses used as landscape plants are a young development, but one that has taken off, if you will excuse the simile, like a prairie fire. Not, however, in seashore gardens, except for the all-important beach grass used as dune protectors. I never connected ornamental grasses with the shore until I saw the Feldman garden on Martha's Vineyard, featured in the "Gardens at the Shore" chapter. Not only do the grasses look perfect in a windy seashore environment, the taller ones can be included in a windbreak.

Festuca glauca
blue fescue

A neat small ornamental grass, no more than 8 inches tall, this is a perfect match for the sea and a delightful contrast to sand. It makes a good ground cover and looks even better as an attractive tuft in a flower bed. It needs sun and good drainage and can take the heat. Zone 3.

Miscanthus sinensis
Japanese silver grass, eulalia grass

This certainly is our oldest landscape grass, used in gardens long before ornamental grasses became a fashion. It's easy to use, grows in clumps, and makes a friendly hedge or a windbreak at the shore. There are dozens of cultivars, more every year. 'Cabaret' grows 6 to 8 feet tall in a weeping cascade with pink flowers that lighten to creamy white. Zones 7 to 10. This species and some other cultivars are hardy to zone 5.

Muhlenbergia capillaris

Phormium tenax

Stipa tenuissima

Muhlenbergia capillaris
muhly grass

Native to the islands off the North Carolina coast, as well as from Florida to Texas. Plantsman Allan Armitage, a University of Georgia professor of horticulture, says that when the pinkish flowers appear in summer, this grass is a showstopper. Zones 7 to 10. *Muhlenbergia filipes*, purple muhly or sweetgrass, grows well in sand and light rocky soils and is a good choice for seashore gardens. Zones 7 to 9.

Phormium tenax
New Zealand flax

Only two species, native, as the name says, to New Zealand. The dramatic colors of the irislike leaves make this a stunning specimen plant. It grows well in sand and at the coast. Depending on the size of your property, you may prefer a compact cultivar, at 3 to 5 feet, over the species, which can reach 10 feet high and wide. Zones 8 to 10.

Stipa tenuissima
Mexico feather grass

I fell in love with a container of this grass last summer, although I didn't know anything about it. It looked just beautiful in the front of my garden all summer, and when it was still there, looking not seriously the worse for wear, in spring, I finally realized it wasn't still alive. In California, it shows signs of being a troublesome weed, so if it is hardy where you live, take this into consideration. Zones 7 to 10.

Viewing Coastal Gardens and Habitats

The gardens and viewing areas listed here are open to the public and provide information and often excellent sites for viewing coastal plant communities and cultivated gardens along the shore. Some addresses shown here are for information centers.

WEST COAST

Washington

Ebey's Landing National Historical Reserve
162 Cemetery Road
Coupeville, WA 98239
(360) 678-6084
www.nps.gov/ebla/index.htm

Jardin du Soleil
3932 Sequim Dungeness Way
Sequim, WA 98382
(360) 582-0846
www.jardindusoleil.com
www.lavenderfestival.com

Lake Ozette boardwalk to Cape Alava
Hoko-Ozette Road
Sekiu, WA 98381
Lake Ozette Ranger Station: (206) 963-2725

Long Beach Peninsula
Highway 101 at Highway 103
Seaview, WA 98644
(360) 642-2400
www.funbeach.com/

Makah Cultural and Research Center
P.O. Box 160
Neah Bay, WA 98357
(360) 645-2711
www.makah.com/mcrchome.htm

Meerkerk Rhododendron Gardens
3531 Meerkerk Lane
Whidbey Island
Greenbank, WA 98253
(360) 678-1912
www.meerkerkgardens.org

Olympic National Park
600 East Park Avenue
Port Angeles, WA 98362-6798
Sites include the Hoh Rain Forest, Hurricane
    Ridge, Lake Quinault, and Rialto Beach.
(360) 565-3130
www.nps.gov/olym/index.htm

Port Angeles Visitor Information Center
121 East Railroad Avenue
Port Angeles, WA 98362
(360) 452-2363
www.portlangeles.org

Purple Haze Lavender Farm
180 Bell Bottom Road
Sequim, WA 98382
(360) 683-1714
www.purplehazelavender.com

San Juan Island National Historic Park
650 Mullis Street, Suite 100
Friday Harbor, WA 98250
(360) 378-2902
www.nps.gov/sajh/index.htm

Oregon

Azalea Park Gardens
898 Elk Drive Brookings, OR 97415
(541) 469-1100
www.brookings.or.usparks%20and%20recreation/
    Azalea%20Park/Azalea%20Park.htm

Cape Meares Lighthouse and Octopus Tree
Cape Meares Loop, 10 miles west of Tillamook
Oceanside, OR
(800) 551-6949
www.oregonstateparks.org/park_181.php

Cape Perpetua Visitors Center and
    Cape Perpetua Scenic Area
2400 Highway 101
Yachats, Oregon 97498
(541) 547-3289
www.fs.fed.us/r6/siuslaw/recreation/
    tripplanning/capeperpetua/events/index.shtml

Connie Hansen Garden
1931 NW 33rd Avenue
Lincoln City, OR 97367
(541) 994-6338
www.conniehansengarden.com.

Darlingtonia Wayside
Mercer Lake Road
Florence, OR
(800) 551-6949
www.oregonstateparks.org/park_115.php

Flora Pacifica
15447 Ocean View Drive
Brookings, OR 97415
(541) 469-9741
www.florapacifica.com/

Heceta Head Lighthouse State Scenic Viewpoint
US Highway 101, milepost 178
Florence, OR 97439
(541) 547-3416
www.oregonstateparks.org/park_124.php

Oregon Dunes National Recreation Area
    and Visitor Center
855 Highway Avenue
Reedsport, OR 97467
(541) 271-3611
www.fs.fed.us/r6/siuslaw/recreation/
    tripplanning/oregondunes/

Redwood Grove Nature Trail
Chetco River and Alfred A. Loeb State Park
North Bank Chetco River Road
Brookings, OR 97415
(541) 469-2021
www.oregonstateparks.org/park_72.php

Shore Acres State Park Gardens
Cape Arago Highway
Coos Bay, OR 97420
(541) 888-3732
www.shoreacres.net

Siletz Bay Nature Trail
Lincoln City Visitor and Convention Bureau
801 SW Highway 101, Suite 1
Lincoln City, OR 97367
(541) 996-1274
www.oregoncoast.org/pages/about-lc.html

Umpqua Lighthouse
460 Lighthouse Rd
Winchester Bay, OR 97467
(541) 271-4118
www.oregonstateparks.org/park_121.php

Yaquina Head Lighthouse and
    Yaquina Head Outstanding Natural Area
750 Lighthouse Drive
Newport, OR 97365
(541) 574-3116
www.mtnvisions.com/QTVR/OreQTVR/
    CenCoast/YaqQTVR.html

California

Alice Keck Park Memorial Gardens
Santa Barbara Street
Santa Barbara, CA 93101

Azalea State Reserve
15336 Highway 101
Trinidad, CA 95570
(707) 488-2041
www.parks.ca.gov/default.asp?page_id=420

Mendocino Coast Botanical Gardens
18220 North Highway 1
Fort Bragg, CA 95437
(707) 964-4352
www.gardenbythesea.org/

Point Reyes National Seashore
1 Bear Valley Road
Point Reyes Station, CA 94956
(415) 464-5100
www.nps.gov/pore/

Prairie Creek Redwoods State Park
Newton B. Drury Scenic Parkway
Orick, CA 95555
(707) 464-6101
www.parks.ca.gov/?page_id=415
San Luis Obispo Botanical Garden
Highway 1 in El Chorro Regional Park
P.O. Box 4957
San Luis Obispo, CA 93403
(805) 546-3501
www.slobg.org/

Sherman Library and Gardens
2647 East Pacific Coast Highway
Corona del Mar, CA 92625
(949) 673-2261
www.slgardens.org/

Sierra Azul Nursery and Gardens
2660 East Lake Avenue (Highway 152)
Watsonville, CA 95076
831-763-0939
www.sierraazul.com/

Wrigley Memorial and Botanical Gardens
Catalina Island Conservancy
P.O. Box 2739
Avalon, CA 90704
(310) 510-2595
www.catalina.com/memorial.html

EAST COAST

Massachusetts

Cape Cod National Seashore
99 Marconi Station Site Road
Wellfleet, MA 02667
(508) 349-3785
www.nps.gov/caco/index.htm

Rhode Island

Block Island Greenway Trails
Block Island, RI
www.blockislandguide.com/nature.html

New York

Fire Island National Seashore
120 Laurel Street
Patchogue, NY 11772
(631) 289-4810
www.nps.gov/fiis/index.htm

Madoo Conservancy (Robert Dash garden)
618 Sagg Main Street
Sagaponack, NY 11962
(631) 537-8200
www.madoo.org

Planting Fields Arboretum State Historic Park
1395 Planting Fields Road
Oyster Bay, NY 11771
(516) 922-9200
www.plantingfields.org/

New Jersey

Hereford Inlet Lighthouse Gardens
First and Central Avenues
North Wildwood, NJ 08260
(609) 522-4520
www.herefordlighthouse.org/main.htm

Island Beach Northern Natural Area
    and Southern Natural Area
Island Beach State Park
Seaside Park, NJ
www.state.nj.us/dep/parksandforests/
    parks/island.html

Sandy Hook and Gateway National Recreation
    Area
Fort Hancock, NJ 07732
www.nps.gov/gate/
www.nps.gov/gate/shu/shu_home.htm

Delaware

Delaware Seashore State Park
39345 Inlet Road
Rehoboth Beach, DE 19971
(302) 227-2800
DNREC Online, www.destateparks.com/dssp/
    dssp.asp

Maryland

Assateague Island National Seashore
7206 National Seashore Lane
Berlin, MD 21811
(410) 641-1441
www.nps.gov/asis/

Chesapeake Bay
Chesapeake Bay Program Office
410 Severn Avenue, Suite 109
Annapolis, MD 21403
(800) your-bay<sc>
www.chesapeakebay.net/index.cfm

Home and Garden Information Center
12005 Homewood Road
Ellicott City, MD 21042
(410) 531-1757
www.hgic.umd.edu/

Jug Bay Natural Area
16000 Croom Airport Road
Upper Marlboro, MD 20772
(301) 627-6074
www.pgparks.com/places/parks/jugbay.html

Virginia

First Landing Seashore State Park
2500 Shore Drive
Virginia Beach, VA 23451 -1415
(757) 412-2300
www.dcr.state.va.us/parks/1stland.htm

North Carolina

Cape Hatteras National Seashore
1401 National Park Drive
Manteo, NC 27954
(252) 995-4474
www.nps.gov/caha/index.htm

Cape Lookout National Seashore
131 Charles Street
Harkers Island, NC 28531
(252) 728-2250
www.nps.gov/calo/index.htm

South Carolina

Brookgreen Gardens
1931 Brookgreen Drive
Murrells Inlet, SC 29576
(843) 235-6000
www.brookgreen.org/index2.html

Cypress Gardens
3030 Cypress Gardens Road
Moncks Corner, SC 29455
(843) 553-0515
www.cypressgardens.org/

Georgia

Cumberland Island National Seashore
113 Saint Marys Street
Saint Marys, GA 31558
(877) 860-6787; (912) 882-4335
www.nps.gov/cuis/index.htm

Florida

Amelia Island Welcome Center
102 Centre Street
Fernandina Beach, FL 32034
(800)-2amelia<SC>
(904) 277-1221
www.ameliaisland.org

Canaveral National Seashore Information Center
7611 South Atlantic Avenue
New Smyrna Beach, FL 32169
(321) 267-1110
www.nps.gov/cana/index.htm

Extension Services

Extension services often have horticultural divisions. For more information on coastal-area plants and events, contact your state or county extension service, often connected with the universities. Extension service websites often provide contact information for county programs.

WEST COAST

Washington State University Extension
Hulbert 411
Washington State University
Pullman, WA, 99164-6248
(509) 335-2837
http://ext.wsu.edu/

Oregon State University Extension
101 Ballard Hall, Oregon State University
Corvallis, OR 97331-3606
(541) 737-2713
http://extension.oregonstate.edu/index.php

University of California Cooperative
    Extension Service
4800 Cesar Chavez Avenue
Los Angeles, CA 90022
(323) 260-2267
http://celosangeles.ucdavis.edu/

EAST COAST

University of Massachusetts Extension
Draper Hall
    40 Campus Center Way
    University of Massachusetts
    Amherst, MA 01003-9244
(413) 545-2716
www.umassextension.org/index.html

University of Rhode Island Cooperative
    Extension Education Center
3 East Alumni Avenue
Kingston, RI 02881
(401) 874-2900
www.uri.edu/ce/index1.html

Connecticut Cooperative Extension System
University of Connecticut
1376 Storrs Road, Unit 4134
Storrs, CT 06269-4134
(860) 486-1987
www.canr.uconn.edu/ces/

Cornell University Cooperative Extension Service
365 Roberts Hall
Cornell University
Ithaca, NY 14853-5905
(607) 255-2237
www.cce.cornell.edu/

Rutgers Cooperative Research and Extension
Cook College
Rutgers, The State University of New Jersey
88 Lipman Drive
New Brunswick, NJ 08901-8525
(732) 932-9306
www.rcre.rutgers.edu/

Delaware Cooperative Extension
Research and Education Center, Sussex County
   16684 County Seat Highway
   Georgetown, DE 19947
(302) 856-7303
http://ag.udel.edu/extension/index.php

Maryland Cooperative Extension
1202 Symons Hall
University of Maryland
College Park, MD 20742-5551
(301) 405-2907
www.agnr.umd.edu/MCE/index.cfm

Virginia Cooperative Extension
Virginia Tech
101 Hutcheson Hall (0402)
Blacksburg, VA 24061
(540) 231-5299
www.ext.vt.edu/

North Carolina Cooperative Extension Service
NC A&T State University, Coltrane Hall
   Greensboro, NC 27411
(336) 334-7956
   www.ces.ncsu.edu/

North Carolina Cooperative Extension Service
NC State University, Raleigh, NC 27695
(919) 515-2011

Clemson University Cooperative Extension
103 Barre Hall
Clemson University
Clemson, SC 29634-0101
(864) 656-3382
www.clemson.edu/extension/

Georgia Cooperative Extension
University of Georgia
147 Cedar Street, Conner Hall
Athens, GA 30602
(706) 542-3824
www.caes.uga.edu/extension/

Florida Cooperative Extension Service
University of Florida
P.O. Box 110210
   Gainesville FL 32611-0210
   (352) 392-1761
www.ifas.ufl.edu/extension/ces.htm

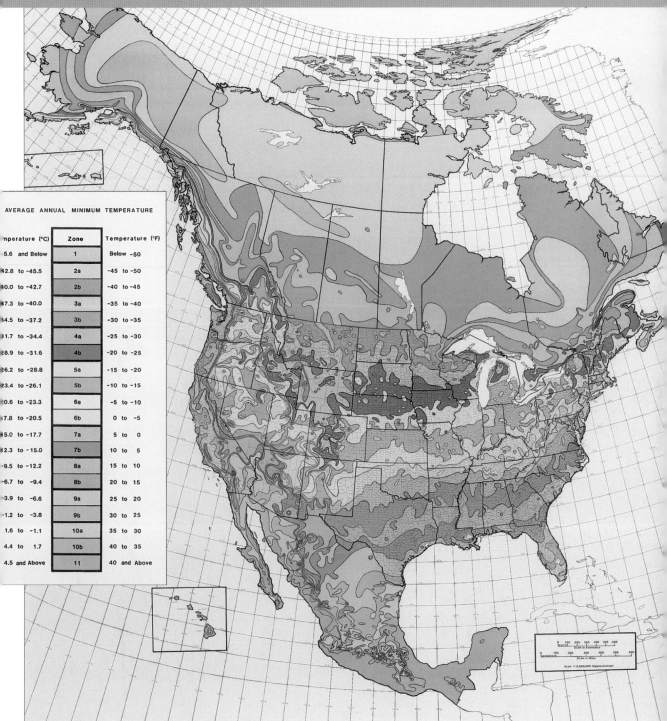

USDA PLANT HARDINESS ZONE MAP

AVERAGE ANNUAL MINIMUM TEMPERATURE

Temperature (°C)	Zone	Temperature (°F)
5.6 and Below	1	Below −50
42.8 to −45.5	2a	−45 to −50
40.0 to −42.7	2b	−40 to −45
47.3 to −40.0	3a	−35 to −40
34.5 to −37.2	3b	−30 to −35
31.7 to −34.4	4a	−25 to −30
28.9 to −31.6	4b	−20 to −25
26.2 to −28.8	5a	−15 to −20
23.4 to −26.1	5b	−10 to −15
20.6 to −23.3	6a	−5 to −10
17.8 to −20.5	6b	0 to −5
15.0 to −17.7	7a	5 to 0
12.3 to −15.0	7b	10 to 5
9.5 to −12.2	8a	15 to 10
6.7 to −9.4	8b	20 to 15
3.9 to −6.6	9a	25 to 20
1.2 to −3.8	9b	30 to 25
1.6 to −1.1	10a	35 to 30
4.4 to 1.7	10b	40 to 35
4.5 and Above	11	40 and Above

Bibliography

Brenzel, Kathleen Norris, ed. *Western Landscaping Book*. Menlo Park, CA: Sunset, 1997.

Bryant, David, and George Davidson. *Georgia's Amazing Coast*. Athens, Georgia: University of Georgia Press, 2003.

Cullina, William. *Native Trees, Shrubs & Vines: A Guide to Using, Growing, and Propagating North American Woody Plants*. Boston; Houghton Mifflin, 2002.

Dash, Robert. *A Walk Through Madoo*. Sagaponack, NY: Madoo Conservancy, 2004.

Dash, Robert. *Notes from Madoo*. Boston: Houghton Mifflin, 2000.

DNREC Online. "Beachgrass Planting and Dune Preservation." www.dnrec.state.de.us/DNREC2000/Divisions/Soil/Beachgrass/gras.htm.

Donohue, Greg. "Against All Odds: A Lighthouse Looks to the Future." www.montauklighthouse.com/donohue.htm.

Flemer III, William. *Nature's Guide to Successful Gardening and Landscaping*. New York: Thomas Y. Crowell, 1972.

Foley, Daniel J. *Gardening by the Sea from Coast to Coast*. Orleans, MA: Parnassus Imprints/Chilton, 1965.

Holmes, Roger. *Taylor's Guide to Ornamental Grasses*. Boston: Houghton Mifflin, 1997.

Jenkins, Mary Zuazua. *National Geographic Guide to America's Public Gardens: 300 of the Best Gardens to Visit in the U.S. and Canada.* Washington, DC: National Geographic Society, 1998.

Lowry, Judith Larner. *Gardening with a Wild Heart.* Berkeley and Los Angeles: University of California Press, 1999.

Menninger, Edwin A. *Seaside Plants of the World.* New York: Hearthside Press, 1964.

Meredith, Ted Jordan. *Bamboo for Gardens*, Portland, OR: Timber Press, 2001.

Munz, Philip A. *Introduction to Shore Wildflowers of California, Oregon, and Washington.* Berkeley: University of California Press, 2003.

Petry, Loren C. *A Beachcomber's Botany.* Chatham, MA: Chatham Conservation Foundation, 1963.

Randall, John M., and Janet Marinelli, eds. *Invasive Plants.* Brooklyn, NY: Brooklyn Botanic Garden, 1996.

Oakley, Myrna. *Oregon: Off the Beaten Path.* 7th ed. Guilford, CT: Globe Pequot Press, 2005.

Oakley, Myrna. *Washington: Off the Beaten Path.* 6th ed. Guilford, CT: Globe Pequot Press, 2005.

Raver, Anne. "Ill Winds Improve the View." *The New York Times*, 23 March 2004.

Reid, Giorgina. *How to Hold Up a Bank.* Cranbury, NJ: A.S. Barnes, 1969.

Schmidt, Marjorie G. *Growing California Native Plants.* Berkeley: University of California Press, 1980.

Schmidt, R. Marilyn. *Gardening on the Eastern Seashore.* Rev. ed. Chatsworth, NJ: Pine Barrens Press, 2005.

Snodsmith, Ralph. *The Tri-State Gardener's Guide*. Nashville, TN: Cool Springs Press, 2001.

Snover, A. K., E. L. Miles, and Climate Impacts Group. *Rhythms of Change: Climate Impacts on the Pacific Northwest*. Cambridge, Massachusetts: MIT Press, in review.

Tenenbaum, Frances, ed. *Taylor's Guide to Seashore Gardening*. Boston: Houghton Mifflin, 1996.

USDA Plant Hardiness Zone Map. www.usna.usda.gov/Hardzone/ushzmap.html.

Watson, Lyall. *Heaven's Breath: A Natural History of the Wind*. New York: William Morrow, 1984.

Index

Page numbers in *italic* indicate illustrations.

Acacia cultriformis, 101, 110
Acacia longifolia, 110
Acca sellowiana, 110, *111*
Acer buergerianum, 34
Acer platanoides, 62
Acer pseudoplatanus, 62, 110, *111*
Achillea, *86*, 143
Achillea 'Coronation Gold', *143*
Achillea millefolium 'Paprika', *143*
Aegopodium podagraria, 62, 104
"Against All Odds: A Lighthouse Looks to the Future," 59
Agapanthus, 101
Ailanthus altissima, 62
Ajuga genevensis, 104
Ajuga reptans, *10–11*
alder, red. *See Alnus rubra*
Aleppo pine. *See Pinus halepensis*
Allium, 85
Alnus rubra, *111*
Amelanchier, 112
Amelanchier ×*grandiflora*, *53*
American beach grass. *See Ammophila breviligulata*
American holly. *See Ilex opaca*
Ammophila arenaria, 56, 153
Ammophila breviligulata, 49, 63, 96, 153, *154*
    transplanting, 56
anemones, 86
annuals, *103*
Arbutus menziesii, *19*, 101, 112, *113*
Arctostaphylos, 101
Arctostaphylos patula, 112, *113*
Arctostaphylos uva-ursi, 104, 112, *113*
Arctotheca calendula, 63
Armeria maritima, 103, 145
Armeria maritima 'Splendens, *144*

Artemisia californica, 103
Artemisia 'Powis Castle', *144*, 145
Artemisia schmidtiana, 145
Artemisia stelleriana, 104
Artemisia stelleriana 'Silver Brocade', *80*
Asclepias tuberosa 'Gay Butterflies', *144*, 145
Astilbe, *36*
Astilbe japonica 'Deutschland', *82*
Atriplex canescens, 114
Austin, David, roses, 101
Australian pine. *See Casuarina*
autumn olive. *See Elaeagnus umbellata*

Baccharis halimifolia, 114
Baccharis pilularis, 103
bald cypress. *See Taxodium distichum*
balloon flower. *See Platycodon grandiflorus*
bamboo, *72*, 151–153
    arrow. *See Pseudosasa japonica*
    common. *See Bambusa vulgaris*
    Japanese timber. *See Phyllostachys bambusoides*
    temple. *See Semiarundaria fastuosa*
Bambusa vulgaris, *152*, 153
Baptisia australis, *145*
barberry. *See Berberis thunbergii*
bayberry. *See Myrica pensylvanica*
    California. *See Myrica californica*
    southern. *See Myrica cerifera*
beach aster. *See Erigeron glaucus*
beach grass, American. *See Ammophila breviligulata*
beach grasses, 49, 54, 56
beach heather. *See Hudsonia tormentosa*
beach plum. *See Prunus maritima*
beach rose. *See Rosa rugosa*
beach wormwood. *See Artemisia stelleriana*
"Beachgrass Planting and Dune Preservation," 56
bearberry. *See Arctostaphylos uva-ursi*
beetlebung. *See Nyssa sylvatica*

Belamcanda, 82

Belgian fence, *42*

Bell garden, *10*

bellflower. *See Campanula takesimana; see also Campanula* 'Kent Belle'

belts, exposure, 55

Berberis thunbergii, 61, 62, 104

Betula nigra, 34

birch, river. *See Betula nigra*

bittersweet, oriental. *See Celastrus orbiculatus*

bitter switchgrass. *See Panicum amarum* 'Dewey Blue'

black gum. *See Nyssa sylvatica*

black spruce. *See Picea mariana*

blue fescue. *See Festuca glauca*

Blue garden, *11*

blue mist. *See Caryopteris ×clandonensis*

blue oat grass. *See Helictotrichon sempervirens*

bluebeard. *See Caryopteris ×clandonensis*

blueberry, highbush. *See Vaccinium corymbosum*

bluffs and cliffs, 20–21, 56–59, *58,* 103

boxwood. *See Buxus*

Brooklyn Botanic Garden, 61, 63

broom. *See Genista lydia; Genista pilosa*

buckwheat, chalk. *See Eriogonum latifolium*

burning bush. *See Euonymus alatus*

Busby, Peter, 70

butterfly weed. *See Asclepias tuberosa*

Buxus, 74

cabbage palm. *See Sabal palmetto*

California bayberry. *See Myrica californica*

California coastal regions, 20–22

California Exotic Pest Plant Council, 63

California laurel. *See Umbellularia californica*

California poppy. *See Eschscholzia californica*

California sagebrush. *See Artemisia californica*

Calluna, 101, 104

Calluna vulgaris, 53, 66, 68, *114*

Camiccia, Terry and Ralph, 72

Camiccia garden, *39, 72–74, 103*

Campanula 'Kent Belle', *80*

Campanula takesimana, 104

Campbell garden, *12, 40, 107*

camphor tree. *See Cinnamomum camphora*

candytuft. *See Iberis sempervirens*

capeweed. *See Arctotheca calendula*

Carolina jasmine. *See Gelsemium sempervirens*

Carpobrotus chilensis, 62, 63

Carya ovata, 34

Caryopteris ×clandonensis 'Longwood Blue', *115*

Casuarina, 62

catmint. *See Nepeta ×faassenii*

Ceanothus, 70

Ceanothus americanus, 116

Ceanothus 'Concha', *115*

cedar

    eastern red. *See Juniperus virginiana*

    Port Orford. *See Chamaecyparis lawsoniana*

    salt. *See Tamarix ramosissima*

    white. *See Thuja occidentalis*

Celastrus orbiculatus, 61–62

Chamaecyparis lawsoniana, 101, *116*

Chasmanthium latifolium, 96, *97*

Chassé, Patrick, 23

Chinese elm. *See Ulmus parvifolia*

Chinese privet. *See Ligustrum sinense*

Christmas berry. *See Heteromeles salicifolia*

Chrysanthemum, 84

Churchill, Richard, 53

Cinnamomum camphora, 34

Cistus salviifolius, 104

Clematis, 94

Clematis 'Paul Farges', *83*

Clemson University, 35

Clethra alnifolia, 117

Clethra alnifolia 'Hummingbird', *117*

Climate Impacts Group, 16

climate zones, 22–24. *See also* hardiness zones

coastal regions, described

    California, 20–22

    Northeast, 22–24

    Pacific Northwest, 16–20

    South Atlantic, 25–29

common thrift. *See Armeria maritima*

composting, 47

Comptonia peregrina, 104, *117*

coneflower, purple. *See Echinacea purpurea*

conifers for seashore gardens, 101

Corona del Mar garden, *58*

Coronilla, 62

Coronilla varia, 104

Cortaderia jubata, 63

Cortaderia selloana, 62

Cotoneaster, 104

coyote bush. *See Baccharis pilularis*

Creagh garden, *10*

Cross, Connie, design, *23, 32*

crown vetch. *See Coronilla*

Cryptomeria japonica, 101, 118
Cryptomeria japonica 'Cristata', *118*
Cryptomeria japonica 'Lobbii', 118
Cullina, William, 65, 119, 122, 127
Cupressus macrocarpa, 21, 75–76, *76*, *118*, 119
cypress
       bald. *See Taxodium distichum*
       Lawson. *See Chamaecyparis lawsoniana*
       palm. *See Taxodium ascendens*
Cytisus scoparius, 62, *62*, 63

Dash, Robert, 34, 88–89
Dash garden, *88–90*
dawn redwood. *See Metasequoia glyptostroboides*
daylily. *See Hemerocallis*
Delairea odorata, 63
Delaware Department of Natural Resources and
    Environmental Control (DNREC), 56
Delphinium, 83, 84, *85*
Dennstaedtia punctilobula, 104
dianthus, *36*
Dickson garden, *9*, *37*
Dixon garden, *91–93*
Donahue, Greg, 59
dunes, sand, 29, *46*, 46–49, 53–56, 101
dune sunflower. *See Helianthus debilis*

eastern red cedar. *See Juniperus virginiana*
Easton, Valerie, 20, 102
Echinacea purpurea, *146*, 147
eelgrass. *See Zostera*
Elaeagnus angustifolia, 62, 63
Elaeagnus commutata, 63, *119*
Elaeagnus umbellata, 62, 63
elm
       Chinese. *See Ulmus parvifolia*
       lacebark. *See Ulmus parvifolia*
Elymus. See Leymus mollis
English holly. *See Ilex aquifolium*
English ivy. *See Hedera helix*
Epstein garden, *33*, *60*
Erica, *45*, 68
Erica carnea 'Springwood White', *53*, *66*
Erigeron glaucus, *103*
Eriobotrya japonica, 44
Eriogonum latifolium, *103*
erosion, 20–21, 59, 103
Erysimum, 102
Escallonia, 101

Eschscholzia californica, *95*, 103
espaliered fence, *43*
Eucalyptus globulus, 62, 63
eulalia grass. *See Miscanthus sinensis*
Euonymus alatus, 62
Euonymus fortunei, 104
Eupatorium, 84
Euphorbia characias, 147
Euphorbia characias subsp. *wulfenii*, *146*
Euphorbia myrsinites, 104
European beach grass. *See Ammophila arenaria*
evening primrose, 84
evergreens, broadleaf, 101
exposure belts, 55

false indigo. *See Baptisia australis*
Feldman, Gretchen and Sam, 86
Feldman garden, *2–3*, *86–87*, *155*
fern, hay-scented. *See Dennstaedtia punctilobula*
fern, sweet. *See Comptonia*
Festuca glauca, 102, *155*
Festuca glauca 'Elijah Blue', *96*, *97*
firethorn. *See Pyracantha*
Flaherty, Robert, 50
flax, New Zealand. *See Phormium tenax*
Flemer, William, III, 48, 110
Florida Department of Environmental Protection,
    55
Foley, Daniel J., *9*, 12, 31, 114, 117
fountain grass. *See Pennisetum alopecuroides*
freezing-thawing cycles, 23
French, Lew, 80
Fruchtman garden, *38*, *64*

Gardening by the Sea from Coast to Coast (Foley), 9,
    31, 114
Gardening on the Eastern Seashore (Schmidt), 55
gardening resources, 25, 117, 158–164
Gardening with a Wild Heart (Lowry), 20
Gardening with Wildflowers (Tenenbaum), 65
GardenWeb, 25, 99
Gaultheria shallon, 69, 101, *119*
Gaura lindheimeri, 86
Gelsemium sempervirens, *142*
Genista lydia, *120*, 121
Genista pilosa, 104
germander. *See Teucrium chamaedrys*
German ivy. *See Delairea odorata*
Gleditsia triacanthos, *45*, *120*, 121

golden rain tree. *See Koelreuteria paniculata*
Goldfield, Cady, 95–96, 151
goutweed. *See Aegopodium podagraria*
grape, wild, *36*
grass
    dune. *See Ammophila breviligulata*
    eulalia. *See Miscanthus sinensis*
    Japanese silver. *See Miscanthus sinensis*
grasses
    beach, approved, 49
    coastal landscape, 96–98, 151–157
    dune, 55–56, 153–154
    ornamental, 155–157
ground covers, 104
groundsel tree. *See Baccharis halimifolia*
guava, pineapple. *See Acca sellowiana*
gum, black. *See Nyssa sylvatica*
gum, sour. *See Nyssa sylvatica*
Guthrie, George, 101

Haag, Richard, and Steve Shramm, design, *66*, *70–71*
Harbor House Inn garden, *21*
hardiness zones, 15–17, 109, *165*
hay, salt-marsh, 51
hay-scented fern. *See Dennstaedtia punctilobula*
heath. *See Erica*
heather. *See Calluna*
heather, beach. *See Hudsonia tormentosa*
Heaven's Breath: A Natural History of the Wind
    (Watson), 31
Hebe, 72, 74, 121
Hebe speciosa 'Violacea', *120*
Hedera helix, *62*, 63
Helianthus annuus, *44*
Helianthus debilis, 55
Helictotrichon sempervirens, 48, 96, 97
Hemerocallis, *37*, *147*
Hemerocallis 'Stella de Oro', *146*
herbs, 100, 104, *105*, *137*
Heteromeles salicifolia, 101, 121
Heteromeles salicifolia var. *cerina*, *121*
Hewitt garden, *22*
hickory. *See Carya ovata*
highbush blueberry. *See Vaccinium corymbosum*
hillside planting, 53
Hippophae rhamnoides, 122
Hoff, John F., design, *12*, *40*, *103*, *105*, *107*

holly
    American. *See Ilex opaca*
    English. *See Ilex aquifolium*
    yaupon. *See Ilex vomitoria*
honey locust. *See Gleditsia triacanthos*
Hood/Logan garden, *8*, *51*
Horticopia.com, 117
Horticulture, 20, 35, 78, 102
Hough, Henry Beetle, 135
How to Hold Up a Bank (Reid), 59
Hudsonia tormentosa, *122*
Hunt, Ann, 99–100
hurricanes, 31–32, 34
Hydrangea macrophylla, *123*

Iberis sempervirens, *104*
ice plant. *See Carpobrotus chilensis*
Ilex, 101, 124
Ilex aquifolium, 124
Ilex opaca, 124
Ilex opaca 'Canary', 124, *125*
Ilex opaca f. *xanthocarpa*, *108*, 124
Ilex vomitoria, *10*, 34, 124, *125*
Ilex vomitoria 'Nana', *37*
indigo, false. *See Baptisia australis*
invasive plants, 61, 62, 104
Invasive Plants (Brooklyn Botanic Garden), 61, 63
Ipomoea pes-caprae, 55
Iris ensata, *24*, 86, 87

Japanese barberry. *See Berberis thunbergii*
Japanese black pine. *See Pinus thunbergii*
Japanese honeysuckle. *See Lonicera japonica*
Japanese iris. *See Iris ensata*
Japanese mock orange. *See Pittosporum tobira*
Japanese silver grass. *See Miscanthus sinensis*
jasmine, Carolina. *See Gelsemium sempervirens*
Joe Pye weed, 84, 86
Joint Institute for the Study of the Atmosphere and
    Ocean, 16
juniper, shore. *See Juniperus conferta*
Juniperus, *10*, 101, 104
Juniperus conferta, 124–126, *125*
Juniperus horizontalis 'Bar Harbor', 124
Juniperus horizontalis 'Blue Rug', 124
Juniperus virginiana, 124
Juniperus virginiana 'Burkii', *125*

Kelley garden, *41*
keyhole view, *40*, 106
kinnikinnick. *See Arctostaphylos uva-ursi*
knife acacia. *See Acacia cultriformis*
Kniphofia, 101
Koelreuteria paniculata, 34, 44
Kurman, Keith, design, *33*

Laburnum, *89*
lacebark elm. *See Ulmus parvifolia*
lady's mantle, *36*
lamb's ear. *See Stachys byzantina*
landslides, 20–21
Larner Seeds, 103
laurel, California. *See Umbellularia californica*
laurel oak. *See Quercus laurifolia*
Lavandula, *36*, 48, 101, 102
Lavatera, 102
lavender. *See Lavandula*
lavender cotton. *See Santolina chamaecyparissus*
Lawson cypress. *See Chamaecyparis lawsoniana*
Legasey home, *28*
Leucanthemum vulgare, *82*
Leymus mollis, 49, 56, *154*
Ligustrum japonica, *37*, *91*
Ligustrum sinense, 62
lilac. *See Syringa vulgaris*
Limonium perezii, *40*
Liquidambar, 44
Liriope, *86*
live oak. *See Quercus virginiana*
locust, honey. *See Gleditsia triacanthos*
lodgepole pine. *See Pinus contorta*
Lonicera japonica, 61, 62
loosestrife, purple. *See Lythrum salicaria*
loquat. *See Eriobotrya japonica*
Lowcountry gardening, 25–29, 100
Lowry, Judith Larner, 20, 22, 35, 63, 103
lupine. *See Lupinus*
Lupinus, 103
Lythrum salicaria, 62

Madoo, 88–90
madrona. *See Arbutus menziesii*
magnolia, southern. *See Magnolia grandiflora*
magnolia, sweet bay. *See Magnolia virginiana*
Magnolia grandiflora, 34, 45
Magnolia virginiana, 45
Malus 'Spartan', *66*

Maneri, Bill, design, *41*, *91–92*
manzanita, green. *See Arctostaphylos patula*
maple, sycamore. *See Acer pseudoplatanus*
maple, trident. *See Acer buergerianum*
marram grass. *See Ammophila breviligulata*
McClary garden, *27*
McMorrow, Phyllis, 80
    design, *80–83*
meadow rue. *See Thalictrum flavum*
Metasequoia glyptostroboides, 9
Mexican feather grass. *See Stipa tenuissima*
Meyer, B., garden, *18*, *52*
Meyer, C., garden, *13*, *19*
microclimates, 16, 23–24, 99
Miscanthus, 102
Miscanthus sinensis, *68*, *69*
Miscanthus sinensis 'Cabaret', *155*
Miscanthus sinensis 'Variegata', *37*
Miscanthus sinensis 'Yaku-jima', *13*, *69*, *97*, *98*
mock orange, Japanese. *See Pittosporum tobira*
Monterey cypress. *See Cupressus macrocarpa*
Monterey pine. *See Pinus radiata*
Morris, Glenn, 27
Moss garden, *31*, *33*, 106
moss pink. *See Phlox subulata*
Mounts Botanical Garden, 34
Muhlenbergia capillaris, *156*
Muhlenbergia filipes, 157
muhly grass. *See Muhlenbergia capillaris*
muhly grass, purple. *See Muhlenbergia filipes*
mulch, 50–51
Myrica, 126
Myrica californica, 101, *126*
Myrica cerifera, 101, 126
Myrica pensylvanica, *127*
myrtle, Oregon. *See Umbellularia californica*
myrtle, wax. *See Myrica cerifera*

National Oceanographic and Atmospheric
    Administration (NOAA), 15
native grasses, 56
native plants, 65, 109
native rye grass. *See Leymus mollis*
*Native Trees, Shrubs, & Vines: A Guide to Using, Growing,
    and Propagating North American Woody Plants* (Cullina),
    119, 127
Nature's Guide to Successful Gardening and Landscaping
    (Flemer, III), 48, 110
Nepeta ×*faassenii*, *24*, *45*, 104, *147*

Nepeta 'Six Hills Giant', 147
Nepeta 'Walker's Low', *82*
Nerium oleander, 101, 127
Nerium oleander 'Petite Pink', *127*
Netters garden, *36*
"New American Garden" style, 86
New England Wild Flower Society, 65, 119, 122
New Jersey tea. *See Ceanothus americanus*
New Zealand flax. *See Phormium tenax*
Northeast climate zones, 22–24
North Shore garden, *80–83*
Norway maple. *See Acer platanoides*
Nyssa sylvatica, *128*

oak, laurel. *See Quercus laurifolia*
oak, live. *See Quercus virginiana*
O'Bryan garden, *37*
Oehme, van Sweden & Associates, 86
Oehme, Wolfgang, design, *2–3*, 86
Oenothera, *84*
olive, autumn. *See Elaeagnus umbellata*
Opuntia humifusa, 148
Opuntia littoralis, *148*
Oregon myrtle. *See Umbellularia californica*
oriental bittersweet. *See Celastrus orbiculatus*

Pacific Northwest coastal regions, 16–20
Pacific wax myrtle. *See Myrica californica*
palm, cabbage. *See Sabal palmetto*
palm, windmill. *See Trachycarpus fortunei*
palmettos, *10*
palms, 34, 101. *See also* palm species
pampas grass. *See Cortaderia jubata; Cortaderia selloana*
panic grass. *See Panicum amarum*
Panicum amarum, 49
Panicum amarum 'Dewey Blue', 49, *154*
Panicum virgatum, 102
Panicum virgatum 'Heavy Metal', *97*
Panicum virgatum 'Warrior', *97*
Parthenocissus quinquefolia, *142*, 143
Paulownia tomentosa, 62
Pennisetum alopecuroides, 97
Penstemon digitalis 'Husker's Red', *87*
perennials for seashore gardens, 143–150
Perovskia atriplicifolia, *24*, 86, 148, *149*
Phlox subulata, 104
Phoenix canariensis, 128, *129*
Phormium tenax, 101, *156*
Phragmites australis, 22

Phyllostachys bambusoides, 72
Picea abies, 74
Picea contorta, 101
Picea glauca, 101, 129
Picea glauca 'Arneson's Blue', *129*
Picea mariana, 101, 130
Picea mariana 'Aurea', *130*
pine
    Aleppo. *See Pinus halepensis*
    Japanese black. *See Pinus thunbergii*
    lodgepole. *See Pinus contorta*
    Monterey. *See Pinus radiata*
    shore. *See Pinus contorta*
pineapple guava. *See Acca sellowiana*
Pinus contorta, *130*
Pinus halepensis, *131*
Pinus radiata, 21
Pinus thunbergii, 84, *101*, *131*
Pittosporum tobira, *131*
Pittosporum tobira 'Variegata', 131
Pittosporum tobira 'Wheeler's Dwarf', 131
planting
    hillside, 53
    sand dunes, 29, 47–49, 53
    for wind protection. *See* windbreaks
Platycodon grandiflorus, *149*
Platycodon grandiflorus 'Sentimental Blue', *149*
Polomski, Bob, 35, 38
Port Orford cedar. *See Chamaecyparis lawsoniana*
prickly pear cactus. *See Opuntia littoralis*
princess tree. *See Paulownia tomentosa*
Princeton Nurseries, 48
pruning
    for hurricanes, 34
    for a view, *40*, 106
    for wind, 72
Prunus cerasifera 'Vesuvius', *33*
Prunus maritima, 45, *132*
Pseudosasa japonica, 98, 152
public viewing gardens, 159–162
purple coneflower. *See Echinacea purpurea*
purple leaf plum. *See Prunus cerasifera*
Pyracantha, 101, 133
Pyracantha coccinea 'Mohave', *133*

Quantz garden, *26*
Quercus laurifolia, 34
Quercus virginiana, *26*, 27, 34, *37*, 55, 101, *134*

railroad vine. *See Ipomoea pes-caprae*
Ratway, Gary, design, *33, 36, 106*
Raver, Anne, 32, 34
red alder. *See Alnus rubra*
Redmon, Dorie Eckard, 29, 100
redwood, dawn, 9
Reed-Trench method, 59
reeds, common. *See Phragmites australis*
Reid, Giorgina and Donald, 59
Rhododendron, 10–11
Rhus copallina, 135
Rhus glabra, 135
Rhus typhina, 134–135
Robertson, Sally, 21, 75, 119
Robertson garden, *75–77*
rock rose. *See Cistus salviifolius*
rocks, as wind barriers, 95–96
Roger's Gardens Colorscape, design, *17, 40, 42, 58*
Rosa, 135
Rosa 'American Pillar', 135
Rosa 'Betty Prior', 102, 135
Rosa 'Bonica', 102
Rosa rugosa, 35, 47, 47, 78, 84, *85*, 102, 135
Rosa rugosa 'Alba', *136*
Rosa 'The Fairy', 102
rose, beach. *See Rosa rugosa*
Rose, Christopher, design, *26, 28, 92–93*
rosemary. *See Rosmarinus officinalis*
rosemary, prostrate. *See Rosmarinus officinalis* 'Prostratus'
roses, 102, 135–136
Rosmarinus officinalis, 137
Rosmarinus officinalis 'Arp', *137*
Rosmarinus officinalis 'Prostratus', *53*
Rothrock, Jean, design, *9, 10, 26, 37*
Russian olive. *See Elaeagnus angustifolia*
Russian sage. *See Perovskia atriplicifolia*

Sabal palmetto, 55, *93, 137*
salal. *See Gaultheria shallon*
salt
    damage, 44–45
    removing from soil, 100
    resistant grasses, 98
    tolerance, 44–45
saltbush, four-wing. *See Atriplex canescens*
salt cedar. *See Tamarix ramosissima*
saltmarsh elder. *See Baccharis halimifolia*
salt-marsh hay, 51
Salvia, 101

Salvia leucantha, 48
Salvia ×*sylvestris*, 87
Salvia ×*sylvestris* 'Mainacht', *82*
Sametz garden, *36*
sand, planting in, 47–49
sand dunes, 29, *46–49, 53–56, 101*
Santolina, 101, *104*
Santolina chamaecyparissus, *104*
Schenk, George, 61
Schmidt, R. Marilyn, 45, 55
Schneider, Peter, 135
Schramm, Steve, 16–17, 68, 70
    design, *8, 13, 18, 19, 43, 45, 51, 52, 68–69*
Schramm, Steve, and Richard Haag, design, *66, 70–71*
Scotch broom. *See Cytisus scoparius*
sea buckthorn. *See Hippophae rhamnoides*
sea myrtle. *See Baccharis halimifolia*
sea oats. *See Uniola paniculata*
sea oats, northern. *See Chasmanthium latifolium*
sea pink. *See Armeria maritima*
Sedum acre, 104
Sedum 'Autumn Joy', *66, 142, 150*
Semiarundinaria fastuosa, *152*, 153
Semiarundinaria fastuosa var. *viridis*, 153
serviceberry. *See Amelanchier*
shadbush. *See Amelanchier*
Shank garden, *43*
shore juniper. *See Juniperus conferta*
shore pine. *See Pinus contorta*
shrubs for seashore gardens, 109–141
silver grass, dwarf. *See Miscanthus sinensis*: 'Yaku-jima'
silver mound. *See Artemisia schmidtiana*
silverberry. *See Elaeagnus commutata*
Sinton, Nan, 78, 136
Sinton garden, *78–79*
Sistrunk, Allen, 34
Smetterer garden, *105*
Smith garden, *103*
sour gum. *See Nyssa sylvatica*
South Atlantic coast climate zones, 25–29
South Coast garden, 91–93
southern bayberry. *See Myrica cerifera*
southern live oak. *See Quercus virginiana*
southern magnolia. *See Magnolia grandiflora*
Spartina pectinata, *26*
Spiraea japonica, 60, 61, *142*
spruce, black. *See Picea mariana*
spruce, white. *See Picea glauca*
spurge. *See Euphorbia characias*; *Euphorbia myrsinites*

Stachys, 104

Stachys byzantina, *95*

staghorn sumac. *See Rhus typhina*

Stipa tenuissima, *48*, *157*

stonecrop. *See Sedum acre*

sumac, staghorn. *See Rhus typhina*

summer sweet. *See Clethra alnifolia*

sunflower

annual. *See Helianthus annuus*

dune. *See Helianthus debilis*

sweet bay magnolia. *See Magnolia virginiana*

sweet fern. *See Comptonia peregrina*

sweetgrass. *See Muhlenbergia filipes*

sweetgum. *See Liquidambar*

sweet pepperbush. *See Clethra alnifolia*

switch grass. *See Panicum virgatum*

switch grass, bitter. *See Panicum amarum*

sycamore maple. *See Acer pseudoplatanus*

Sydney golden wattle. *See Acacia longifolia*

Syringa vulgaris, *138*, 139

tamarisk. *See Tamarix ramosissima*

Tamarix ramosissima, 61, *138*, 139

Taxodium ascendens, 34

Taxodium distichum, 34

Taylor, Trudy, 84

Taylor garden, *38*, *84–85*

Taylor's Guide to Seashore Gardening, 27, 67, 103, 135

Teucrium chamaedrys, 104

Teucrium fruticans, *36*

Thalictrum flavum, 84, *85*

thrift, common. *See Armeria maritima*

Thuja occidentalis, 34

thyme. *See Thymus vulgaris*

Thymus, *36*, 104

Thymus ×*citriodorus* 'Aureus', *81*

Thymus vulgaris, *45*

toyon. *See Heteromeles salicifolia*

Trachycarpus fortunei, *138*, 139

trees

for seashore gardens, 109–141

storm resistant, 34

tupelo. *See Nyssa sylvatica*

Ulmus parvifolia, 34, 44

Umbellularia californica, *140*, 141

Uniola paniculata, 49, 55, 154

United States Department of Agriculture Plant Hardiness Zone Map, 15, *165*

Vaccinium corymbosum, *140*, 141

Vaccinium ovatum, 141

Venuti, Bob, design, *24*

Verbena bonariensis, *13*, 103

Veronica, 85

Veronicastrum virginicum 'Fascination', *82*

Viburnum, *36*, 141

Viburnum nudum 'Winterthur', *141*

Viburnum wrightii, *141*

view, *40*, 106

vines for seashore gardens, 142–143

Vineyard Gazette, 135

Vineyard home, *26*

Virginia creeper. *See Parthenocissus quinquefolia*

wallflower. *See Erysimum*

watering, 50–51

waterlilies, 77

Watson, Lyall, 31

Watsonia, 101

wax myrtle. *See Myrica cerifera*

wax myrtle, Pacific. *See Myrica californica*

websites, gardening, 25, 117, 158–164

white cedar. *See Thuja occidentalis*

white spruce. *See Picea glauca*

wild grape, *36*, *85*

wind

effects of, 23, 25, 31–35

pruning for, 72

resistant grasses, 98

studying a site for, 99–100

windbreaks

creating, 35–38, 78, 95–96

examples of, *31–33*, *36–43*, *78–79*, *81–85*, *106–107*

need for, 29, 32, 102

trees and shrubs for, 109–141

windmill palm. *See Trachycarpus fortunei*

wintercreeper. *See Euonymus fortunei*

woodbine. *See Parthenocissus quinquefolia*

woodwaxen. *See Genista lydia*

yaupon holly. *See Ilex vomitoria*

zones

climate, 22–24

hardiness, 15–17, 109, *165*

Zostera, 50